Tell Me Now

The Self-Esteem and Wellness Guide for Girls

by Donna Ternes Wanner

Authors Choice Press

New York Lincoln Shanghai

Tell Me Now
The Self-Esteem and Wellness Guide for Girls

Authors Choice Press
an imprint of iUniverse, Inc.

iUniverse books may be ordered through booksellers or by contacting:

iUniverse
2021 Pine Lake Road, Suite 100
Lincoln, NE 68512
www.iuniverse.com
1-800-Authors (1-800-288-4677)

Originally published by JudyWood Publisher

ISBN-13: 978-0-595-35445-0
ISBN-10: 0-595-35445-9

Printed in the United States of America

ABOUT THE AUTHOR

Donna Ternes Wanner was born in Bismarck, North Dakota. She is fifth in a family of ten. She received her Bachelor of Science Degree from Dickinson State University, Dickinson, North Dakota, and her Master of Education Degree from Lesley College, Cambridge, Massachusetts.

In Donna's words, *"I remember when I was a teenager. Books about growing up were not available. The closest thing to it was an etiquette book in the library. Also, with ten children in my family, along with chores and responsibilities, little time was left for family discussions.*

"My girlfriends and I would get together on Sunday afternoons and share tips about hair, make-up, exercise and, of course, school and friends. The information we shared came from other sources. I also learned, while I was very young, how rewarding it is to work with a group of people to improve the community. I remember my father offering the use of his lumber yard so people could decorate their floats for the 4th of July parade. He would also string Christmas lights on Main Street every December. My mother helped us bake cookies and pies to take to the church rectory on Sunday after services."

In her spare time, Donna enjoys designing creative programs for children, reading, cooking, skiing and walking. She is currently a professional educator and lives in Cheyenne, Wyoming, where she continues to teach, lecture and consult.

I thank you, Mom and Dad Ternes,
    for teaching me that one of the most rewarding gifts in life is reaching out to others.

PREFACE

In 1990 I began a series of self-esteem and wellness classes for pre-teen girls because I sensed there was a need for such classes among my own fourth grade girls.

One day, a young girl in my classroom looked up at me and said, "Mrs. Wanner, will you teach us some of that stuff you know?"

"What stuff?" I asked.

She replied, "You know, that stuff about taking care of yourself."

I laughed, but as days passed, I constantly heard that voice and saw her face. I couldn't forget what she'd said, and as I continued to think about her request, I realized that what she was really asking for was help to feel better about herself.

I started self-esteem and wellness classes once a week after school. They were offered to girls in fourth, fifth, and sixth grades, and so many enrolled that I had to turn some away. What I discovered during the class sessions was amazing.

Sitting in my classroom were sweet, sincere girls just like you. As we talked and shared ideas, the girls became more and more comfortable asking questions because they realized that so many other girls had many of the same concerns they did. Some of the questions asked were:

♥   How do I make friends?

♥   What kinds of foods should I eat in order to stay healthy?

♥   How can I get along with my parents?

♥   My face has so many pimples; how can I get rid of them?

♥   A girl and I want to be friends but she belongs to a group; how do I get to know her?

The list of questions went on and on with questions about peers, friends, school, and family. I realized more than ever that these girls wanted to learn how to help themselves feel good about themselves.

So that's what this book deals with. It addresses the many questions and concerns young girls have today. It's a book about feelings; a book about health; and it's also a book about goals and careers. During your pre-teen years you feel more independent and experience physical changes.

As you read *Tell Me Now*, you'll learn to understand yourself and people around you better. You'll recognize emotions such as pain, joy, fear, hurt, worry, and more. You will also learn what to do with these emotions and how they can help you become a strong and confident human being.

As you read, try to place yourself in each situation, or, you might say, "in someone else's shoes." Think how situations in your life apply to each example and practice the skills that will help you become a good decision maker.

Finally, use the book as a reference guide for your friends and family, as well as yourself.

DEDICATION

I dedicate this book to all my past and present students who have shared their concerns and insights with me, and to the many young girls around the world who seek to be the best that they can be.

TABLE OF CONTENTS

Feeling Good About Yourself

Do you remember a time when you felt great about something you did well? You probably felt like you could do anything. You felt special and important, and very sure of yourself. This confident feeling probably gave you courage to try things you didn't think you could do. It gave you a reason to succeed. Well, this feeling is called self-esteem. It's a word we hear a lot these days.

So, what exactly is it? Self-esteem is the way you feel about yourself. If you like yourself most of the time, you have positive—or high—self-esteem. If you feel negative about yourself or are always putting yourself down, you have low self-esteem.

Those with positive self-esteem are comfortable with themselves. They don't act conceited or give others the impression that they're better than they are, nor do they compete or always wonder what others will think of them. They realize that they are not perfect, but they're okay most of the time with who they are—birthmarks and all.

Many girls today don't feel very good about themselves. Somewhere along the way they have received messages that caused them to feel unimportant or unable to succeed. They were probably put down by their parents, friends, or peers. These negative messages are constant reminders of low self worth. When these messages are very strong, it takes a long time to overcome them and learn how to feel good about who we are. Some girls may even turn to drugs, drop out of school, join gangs, or become pregnant to earn some kind of attention or acceptance. These are harmful actions. Instead, girls can choose more positive ways of dealing with their self-doubt, ways that will help them feel happier about who they are.

Too often girls worry about themselves. They wish they were like someone else or smarter, prettier, or more popular. They may dress or act like another person because they don't like who they are. Sometimes this is normal. But if girls dwell on these issues too long, they eventually forget how important they are.

Self-esteem can make all the difference when setting goals for your future. Positive self-esteem helps you feel in charge of your life and helps you make healthful choices that are right for you. This positive feeling leads you to see a purpose for your future and gives you the confidence when you work hard to attain your goals.

There are ways you can strengthen your self-confidence. You can determine how to have a happy and successful life along with the respect you want. But first let's look at some examples of high and low self-esteem.

A girl with high self-esteem:

acts responsible	"I'll take out the trash."
is proud of her accomplishments	"I've cleaned my own room."
is okay with failure	"I can't get this math problem, but I'll try again."
likes challenges	"I think I'll try out for the school play again."
is willing to help others	"Let me help you with your report."
expresses positive feelings	"I appreciate you letting my friends come over."

A girl with low self-esteem:

puts herself down	"I'm just not good at anything."
feels others don't like her	"I never have any friends."
is easily frustrated	"I hate this stupid painting. I never did like art."
has a hard time expressing positive feelings	"It doesn't make any difference to me. I don't care."
avoids conflict	"I'm not going. I'll run into someone I don't like."
blames others for her faults	"If you wouldn't leave the TV on, I could finish my homework."

So many times we are harder on ourselves than other people are. When we make mistakes we think negative thoughts and stop believing we are capable of succeeding. It is then harder to try again for fear we might fail, which will make us feel bad all over again.

Negative thinking keeps you from listening to your inner self when it tells you what your strengths are. Self-criticism and self-doubt can be more damaging than you realize, often preventing you from feeling strong and confident. These feelings also prevent you from taking healthy risks when choosing your goals.

How Can I Get Into A Positive Mood?

As I said earlier, we tell ourselves many negative messages. So, how can you change negative messages into positive ones?

1. First of all, stay away from negative thinking as much as possible. Try turning a negative thought into a positive one.

> **Example:** "I'm not very good at sports, but I'm great with the computer." When you find yourself failing or unable to do what others can, ask yourself, "What positive thing happened as a result of the negative one?" Ask yourself, "What have I learned from it and how might I handle it differently next time?"

This advice always works for me and it can work for you, too. I think positively about a negative situation I have experienced, which helps me gain the confidence to try again.

2. Allow yourself to make mistakes. Making mistakes is one of the best ways to learn. You were not born knowing everything.

> **Example:** "I bombed the last English test, but I'll study harder for the mid-term."

3. Don't be too hard on yourself. If you need to complain or let off steam, do so, but don't dwell on it forever.

> **Example:** "My best friend didn't ask me to go along to the game, and I'm really upset. Thanks for listening. I'm sure I'll feel better about it tomorrow."

4. Let your parents know if something is bothering you and tell them how they can help. You will feel better if they know.

> **Example:** "Mom, could I talk with you about something I'm worried about?"

You are the only one who can manage your feelings. Stand up to your negative thoughts and let yourself know that you are the one in control—not someone else. Take the responsibility to change your negative thinking.

How To Build Self-Esteem

Building self-esteem is a skill you will use all of your life. Learning how to do this while you are young will make life easier for you throughout your growing years and into adult life. Put the following ideas in motion:

1. **Help people around you.**

You'll feel needed and others will see that you have something to offer. It also shows responsibility and maturity.

2. **Laugh at yourself.**

Laughing at your mistakes once in awhile helps you feel like you don't have to be perfect to like who you are. If you can laugh at your mistakes, others will tease you less.

3. **Be creative.**

We have new inventions and the world is progressing because people used their imaginations and made their dreams a reality. You can do this too.

4. **Set goals and never give up.**

Set short term goals—a day or a week. Set long term goals—a month or a year. Set goals that you can achieve, not goals that are impossible to accomplish. What a feeling of accomplishment and pride you'll have when you meet these goals!

5. **Take care of your body.**

Eat balanced meals and get plenty of rest. Maintain a good exercise program. This will help you reduce stress, feel strong, and think more positively.

6. **Think positive thoughts and take time to talk over negative concerns.**

It is not normal to feel happy all of the time. When something is bothering you, try talking it over with the other person in a positive and honest way. Your parents may be helpful listeners at this time.

7. **Hang in there and have patience.**

If you don't give yourself time and practice, you will never know if you can succeed at what you are trying to do.

8. **Never give up. Never, never.**

If you honestly believe that what you are doing is right and best for you, then do it. And don't let anyone talk you out of it!

9. **Associate with people who support you.**

Most of the time these people will look at the positive you—not the negative. They will also give you honest advice. Don't forget that your family can be a support group as well.

10. **Take reasonable risks.**

Accomplishing something you didn't think you could do can help you feel wonderful.

11. **Find time for yourself.**

A few moments alone can help you think about what's happening and it will also give you time to make wiser decisions. Do something special for yourself once in awhile.

12. **Give someone a compliment.**

It will not only make the person smile, but you too will have a warm feeling inside.

13. **Watch and learn from those you admire.**

You'd be surprised how much you can learn by watching others. Listen to people who are good at what they do.

14. **Remember, bad days never last forever.**

After a day or two, things will turn around, especially if you make an effort to make improvements.

15. **Pretend to be self-confident.**

Smile and act like you're on top of things. Stand up tall; look people in the eye when you are talking. You will not only be sending a positive message to others, but to yourself as well.

Now let's make a list. Try to think of as many personal strengths as possible. If you have trouble thinking of some, have a friend help you. This is also a good way to find out what strengths your friends see in you.

My Personal Strengths

1. _____
2. _____
3. _____
4. _____
5. _____
6. _____
7. _____
8. _____
9. _____
10. _____

Put your list of strengths on a 3" x 5" index card and leave it on your nightstand or dresser. Each morning look into the mirror and read your strengths to yourself out loud. You may want to do this twice a day. Eventually, you will become aware of how special you are and you'll see that you have a lot going for you.

Every few months and at the end of each year, reevaluate your strengths. You may have to change them or add to your list. Your needs and interests may be different each year. What's important is that you continue to remind yourself of your special talents.

What Are Other Ways To Build Self-Esteem?

Friends Help Build Self-Esteem

Friends are going to be very important to you now. Most of your time is spent with kids your age and you will form close relationships with some of them. You'll want a close friend who you can trust and confide in—someone who will listen and who cares about your feelings. This person can be especially helpful when you feel you can't talk with your parents. At times we aren't sure our parents will understand our feelings. Having a friend to talk with helps give you the confidence to make decisions for yourself.

Choosing a friend can be difficult, especially if someone you like belongs to a "clique." This is a social group that excludes other kids. They sometimes dress alike, wear their hair the same way, and go everywhere together. Belonging to a group isn't necessarily bad, unless they bully and boss others around. This is certainly not going to help you feel secure and confident when trying to make your own decisions. You want a friend who respects you and also respects others.

The kind of friend you want is someone who thinks for herself. Someone who values and understands what she wants. She makes her own decisions and doesn't do just what other people want her to do. She likes and respects herself and has respect for others as well. She's fun to be with because she's positive, but not bragging constantly.

Watch kids at school. You will soon notice those who feel good about themselves and those who don't.

Your Family Can Help Build Self-Esteem

When we are young, our self-esteem comes mostly from our family. It starts with the way your parents hold you and how much attention they give you. When they praise you and support you, it makes you feel very accepted. When they put you down or criticize you, it causes you to question your ability.

It's important to have open communication with the family members you live with.

I know it's hard to think of your parents as people you can talk to, especially when they set rules and regulations for you. But you'd be surprised how understanding they can be. Let them know how much you appreciate them for sharing the positive things they see in you. Also let them know how bad you feel when they talk to you negatively. If they yell or are upset, ask if you can sit down together and talk about it in such a way that no one's feelings are hurt, a way in which you can solve the problem or disagreement together. That way you learn from mistakes yet still maintain your respect and self worth.

Remember: Your parents were your age at one time. Parents have to make difficult decisions about their lives, too. Many of them have been through many problems themselves—divorce, the loss of a relative, or problems at work. If they snap at you it may be that they don't mean to. Talking about it together may make them feel better too. Who knows, they may feel proud that you even asked them to talk. It may be that they have some things on their mind but don't know how to approach you about them. Communication often prevents problems from becoming worse.

Unfortunately, some kids don't have a very structured home life. They're confused and don't quite know where they belong or what's right or wrong. Talking with their parents may not even help, or perhaps their parents don't want to talk. If you have a nearby relative, a neighbor you can trust, or a teacher who you can talk with, go to them for advice. Realize how important it is to know what's right and wrong and that your parents' behavior is not your fault. Talking with someone about it can help you learn about values and purpose, even if you can't learn these life lessons in your home.

As we grow older, we sometimes receive mixed messages. Some parents praise or give love only when we do something right, instead of accepting the best we are capable of. They get angry when their children make mistakes and may even scream or yell at them. Other parents accept their children the way they are, as long as they follow the house rules. Try to sort out mixed messages you are receiving from your parents. They may be angry but may not mean to give negative signals. You need to know that it isn't your fault; they may just be confused. Once again, talk with them about it.

Earlier I mentioned that many girls with low self-esteem become pregnant at an early age. Much of the time this happens because girls want to feel as if someone needs them, and they think a baby is the answer. They don't realize how time-consuming and expensive raising a child can be. But when the child is born, reality sets in. Teenage mothers have to stay at home with their babies while their friends are doing things together. And because the new mother doesn't have a good education, she doesn't make enough money to pay for her living expenses. Eventually she feels like the baby is in the way. She may become frustrated and blame the baby for her new feelings. This can lead to child abuse, or many other problems.

Then, professional help is needed. A counselor will usually help the young mother put some focus back into her life. She needs to learn how to feel worthy so she can help her baby grow up in a healthy way.

So you see, it's much like a cycle. If we have good self-esteem, values, and goals, we can help our own children have the same.

Setting Goals

Once again, having a good self-image can help you make wise choices, which helps you attain worthwhile goals. When you focus your time and energy on something meaningful to you, chances are you will be successful. Working toward goals while you are younger also helps you develop a path for later years.

You can start by setting a few short-term goals, such as getting straight A's on your spelling tests or never missing soccer practice. Before setting your short-term goals, think of something you are good at. Write down a goal that you think you will be able to achieve, yet one you will have to work at a little. When you reach your goal, your self-confidence will increase as well. Try setting a few more goals and continue the process. The more accomplishments you have, the better you'll feel.

Next, set long term goals. These could be subjects you plan to take in high school, where you plan to attend college, or even a career you wish to pursue someday. Your short-term goals may even relate to your long-term goals. Short-term goal: to babysit during school years. Long-term goal: to run a child care center. I will discuss more about goals later in this book, but I think you have an idea of how goals and self-esteem work hand in hand in helping develop a more successful you.

When Things Are Not Going Well For You, Try To Keep These In Mind:

1. Be proud of your accomplishments.
2. Take risks, even if you fail.
3. Continue to be creative and use your imagination.
4. Laugh.
5. Help others.
6. Forgive yourself for your mistakes.
7. Be patient.
8. Try to remember that everyone has good and bad days.

What Can I Do If I Don't Feel Better After A Few Weeks?

You may then need to talk with someone. It may be your teacher, school counselor, minister, friend, relative, or someone you trust.

Many schools have counselors or social workers. You could talk with your teacher and ask her to set up a time for you to talk with the school counselor. If it's hard to do this face to face, call her on the telephone. She can help you with the next step.

If you feel you can't talk with anyone and you need help as soon as possible, call a Crisis Line or a Crisis Prevention Hotline (listed in the back of this book). You can call 24 hours a day. Someone will talk with you and offer help. And don't ever be embarrassed to ask for help. We all need help at one time or another.

Self-esteem is not something you pick up at a fast-food restaurant. It is the part of your personality that you have to work on as you grow older. It's what helps you make good decisions about your future. Your self-esteem depends on the work you put into it.

Remember: Focus on your positive side and inner strengths, not on negative thoughts.

Notes

CHAPTER 2

ASSERTIVENESS

Learning how to feel good about who you are is very important. However, learning how to work with people in difficult situations without losing self-respect and respect from others is equally important.

As you grow older, you come in contact with more and more people, all of whom seem to behave a little differently. Some are friendly and very expressive; others are shy or serious. Some always know the right thing to say. Then there are those who start an argument every time they talk with another person.

Much of what we observe in others teaches us how we should behave—at home and in public. We sort out what's appropriate, and not appropriate, so we can use the information when making decisions about our own behavior.

When we watch how others act, we learn from them about what we call "behaviors." We watch how they react when they like or don't like certain things. We notice how they behave toward others when they are happy or mad. We note body language—how they stand, where they focus their eyes, what tone of voice they use, how they use their hands, and their facial expressions.

Learning how to interact with people is not always easy. But it's a skill worth learning because you will use it forever. This skill helps you make friends, work cooperatively with others, and may even help you save your job someday.

You're probably wondering how you can express your opinions, and not cause others to be intimidated or angry. Well, it's called being assertive—taking control of your feelings and expressing them appropriately.

What Does Assertiveness Mean And Why Is It So Important?

Assertiveness means communicating your ideas and feelings in a way that others will listen and not be offended, because they know their feelings are respected, too. When you're assertive you express your feelings without intimidating others or being intimidated yourself.

First, understand that there are three types of behavior: aggressive behavior, assertive behavior, and passive behavior.

Aggressive behavior is easily spotted because the person talks in a way that offends or intimidates others. He or she is seen as bossy and pushy. For example, your friend asks you to share notes from science class with her since she was ill that day. You tell her no because if she wants to get a good grade in class she should take her own notes.

Assertive behavior is saying what you really want to without giving excuses or making the other person angry. It doesn't mean that you're right all the time. It just means you're stating your true feelings, even if they're different from someone else's. An example of this would be telling your friend that you'll go to the movie with her another time, but your Mom needs you at home tonight, using a friendly tone of voice.

Passive behavior is when you do not communicate honestly, and then you feel frustrated because of it. An example of this would be telling a classmate that you will help her with her homework when you don't want to. Later you feel badly about saying yes.

Being assertive allows you to control the ability to express yourself in appropriate ways. Learning how to interact with others is part of feeling good about yourself. Assertiveness means taking responsibility for your wants, needs, and feelings and making them known to others. It is also a way of protecting your rights and respecting the rights of others.

When you let others talk you into doing things you don't want to do, you often feel uncomfortable. After a while, you will feel like people are manipulative and taking advantage of you. You may even be angry and resentful. This is not good for your self-esteem. If you are assertive and feel good about how you handled things it will help raise your self-esteem. And when your needs are met, you feel good and so do the people around you.

Years ago, women were seen as passive; it was part of being "feminine." Men made most decisions at that time and some women didn't question much or express their feelings, because it wasn't considered their place to do so. It was unusual for many women to voice opinions, disagree, or challenge what was said and done because they were not allowed to.

This passivity had a lot to do with the roles women were assigned. For the most part, women stayed home with children and were supported by husbands who also made most decisions. Some women had full or part time jobs, but not many. Women who chose to work probably did so because they were raised by working mothers. They saw their moms leave for work each day while a "nanny" or housekeeper cared for the children. When these young girls became older, they also decided to have careers whether they married or remained single.

This situation is very different today for women in our culture. Women are now seen as "feminine" because they are female. Some continue to stay home and raise their children and others marry and have children, but also work outside the home. They are also involved in serving their communities through volunteer projects. There are also those who choose to remain single and concentrate on their careers or their personal lives.

What has changed today is that women are allowed to express their views openly and be heard. More women are involved in politics and hold leadership roles than ever before in history. This is why knowing how to interact with people is so important. Having good communication skills should be a priority for young girls today. Learning to be assertive can help you become successful.

Becoming assertive is like learning a new sport or learning how to play the piano. You cannot sit down and play a song on the piano the first time. It may even take several lessons before you will be able to play anything. You'll find it easier to play better one day than another. It takes concentration and lots of practice. As you master each lesson and improve, you become more comfortable and will enjoy learning harder songs. You'll be proud of your success.

The same thing happens when you're learning how to be assertive. You must start with easy and simple situations and ease into more difficult ones. It may be difficult at first. Just remember how it was when you learned how to do something for the first time. At the beginning, you made mistakes, but then you were ready to move on to something harder. Be proud of your accomplishments as you practice assertiveness. Don't be hard on yourself by expecting perfection too soon.

How Can I Be Assertive Without Offending Others Or Being Considered Pushy Or Bossy?

1. Speak with a soft, clear tone of voice and keep your comment short. Say the words like you really mean them, but not in a complaining tone. Be sure about how you feel, so you believe in what you are saying. Make your decisions according to what you feel is right and wrong.

2. Look at the person you're talking to. Don't look down or off to the side. Some people find it hard to look right into the eyes of another person the whole time they are talking. Try looking at their

nose, chin, and mouth, along with their eyes, and you and they may feel more comfortable. A pleasant smile may also help.

3.   Sit or stand up straight when speaking. Don't slouch. You may even use simple hand gestures to help get your point across.

Using Assertive, Aggressive, Or Passive Behavior

AGGRESSIVE: JoAnna: Can I borrow your sweater?

Michelle: No way! You'll probably spill something all over it.

(Michelle's comment is a put-down to JoAnna.)

PASSIVE: JoAnna: Can I borrow your sweater?

Michelle: Uh, well, no, I might want to wear it.

JoAnna: But you're not wearing it now, why can't I wear it?

Michelle: Well, okay.

(Michelle avoids saying no to JoAnna, but wishes she would have.)

ASSERTIVE: JoAnna: Can I borrow your sweater?

Michelle: It's my personal rule not to lend my clothes.

JoAnna: C'mon—just once.

Michelle: I don't lend my clothes to anyone.

(Michelle is not putting JoAnna down. She's not even willing to argue with her. She's just taking care of her own rights.)

Practice saying these sentences assertively:

- ♥ I can't go with you tonight. I have a big history test tomorrow. Maybe another time.

- ♥ We are supposed to be working on this project together but you don't show up at the lab very often. Is there something bothering you?

- ♥ I know you would like to see how I did on my math assignment, but I feel it's private and I'd rather keep it to myself.

- ♥ Last time we rented a movie, you chose your favorite. I would like to make a choice once in a while.

Change these passive examples to assertive statements.

1. Well, I guess I would like a hamburger.

_____

2. I guess I could wait for you.

_____

3. Well, . . . ah . . . well . . . maybe.

_____

4. I think I could go now, okay?

_____

5. I can't leave, she might call.

_____

6. I'd better not ask, he might get mad.

_____

7. I could lend you $5.00 even if it is all of my allowance money.

_____

8. I'll help, even though it's my Dad's birthday.

_____

Now write your own assertive statements to respond to the following aggressive situations.

1. A friend tries to talk you into taking drugs.

_____

2. A classmate wants to copy your homework.

_____

3. A group of kids are laughing at your new sneakers.

_____

4. Your best friend is mad at you because you scored higher on a test.

_____

5. Your little brother is always taking things from your room.

_____

6. Your parents blamed you for something you didn't do.

_____

7. The friend who was going to meet you never showed up.

_____

8. A woman just cut in line in front of you at the grocery store.

_____

Suggestions For Becoming Assertive

1.   If you think you need to learn more assertiveness, ask your teacher, school social worker, or the Mom or Dad of a friend to help you. It should be someone you think you can trust. You may even want another friend to join you. Remember: There is always someone around who can either help you or suggest where you can get the help you need. Take advantage of your opportunities.

2. If you need to work on self-control first, because you have a tendency to flare up, do so—even if you do it slowly. You may have to stop every so often and think about your actions—that's great! The payoff will be worth it. If you need to work on self-control, try not to show your anger and do remain calm.

3. Practice your assertiveness with a couple of people you feel comfortable with. Use positive statements first. You may want to try this with a best friend. Then, after a week, try it on your parents. Eventually you will be ready to use it with more difficult people.

4. Don't ever stop using assertive behavior. As you get older you will be able to handle difficult situations with ease. Eventually you will feel in touch with your feelings, wants, and needs and you will

like being assertive because it feels good.

5. Don't talk as if you're accusing the other person. Think how embarrassed you'll feel if they haven't done anything wrong.

6. Try to deal with the issue instead of being angry at the person. You're really trying to talk about the situation you're concerned about, not the person you're talking with.

7. Breathe deeply and try to relax before confronting someone. Count to 10 while breathing. It also helps to take a walk before confronting the person, so you have time to think and calm down.

8. Don't hold your anger in. Express your concern and don't wait too long. Waiting and stewing about it can be very stressful.

Remember: When you use passive or aggressive behavior you lose self-respect. Using assertive behavior helps you maintain self-respect and gain respect from others.

Taking responsibility for your feelings and owning your own problems means you're becoming mature. You'll also notice that people listen to you and take you seriously. Once again, when you're assertive you not only treat others with dignity and respect, but yourself as well.

Notes

Parents

The relationship you have with your parents is probably the most important one you'll have in your life. The love and trust you share with them makes you feel secure and comfortable. It also gives you the confidence to meet other people and feel comfortable and happy with them.

You have to work at having a good relationship with your parents. Maybe you're happy with your relationship with them most of the time, but there are things you wish you could change. The most important thing is to try to understand them.

There are times when you may have to ask your parents if you can discuss certain sensitive issues. It's often hard for parents to talk with you about these issues, because they may feel they don't know the right answers, or you may feel they can't answer your questions. And sometimes they feel more embarrassed than you do. Respect their feelings, but don't let that stop you from communicating with them if they are willing.

How Do I Talk With My Parents?

One way to start having discussions with your parents is to talk with them about a concern that isn't too serious. After a few chats over less important problems, then you will be ready to go to them when more difficult problems develop. You may be scared, embarrassed, or afraid to ask. But you must try. Your parents won't know you need them unless you ask. Most parents understand a lot more than you give them credit for, but you must ask—your parents can't read your mind.

First, ask your parents when they can talk. Try to plan a time when you can talk alone. You can even do this outside your home, which may make your talk more pleasant. Go on a picnic or to the library to look for books together, walk the mall, have ice cream, or visit your church. If your parents can't do it right away, make an appointment with them, just as you would if you were going to the dentist. They will then realize how serious you are.

The time set aside for your talk can be with either or both parents. I believe it's important to have talks with each of them from time to time. In some situations, there is only one parent in the home, but you may even feel closer after talking with your single parent since the two of you are used to working together.

Remember to use good conversation manners when talking with your parents. This means speaking in a cheerful tone and trying to explain what you mean the best way you know how. Don't slouch and look at the floor while talking. When your parents talk, pay attention; don't interrupt, scream, or accuse anyone. Just listen. Listening is a part of conversation, too. If you don't understand something, ask them to repeat it or explain it. You might even repeat what they said to you and see if you heard them correctly. Listening gives you information and helps you learn.

How Do I Start?

"Mom (or Dad), I really need to talk to you about something."

"Mom (or Dad), I'm scared to tell you this, but . . ."

"Mom (or Dad), I hope you won't be mad, but . . ."

"Mom (or Dad), how would you handle this situation?"

It may feel a little uncomfortable at first, but the more you do it the easier it will be for both of you. It's important that you let your parents know your true feelings, because they may not have a clue about what's bothering you. You may be surprised that your parents want to help you. They may be just as afraid to talk as you are.

Let your parents know that even if they don't have an answer for you, the time they spend talking with you means a lot to you. This will make it much easier to talk with them the next time you have a problem or concern.

Throughout my teaching years, students have asked me many questions about problems they have had dealing with their parents. Some of the most common are:

What Do My Parents Really Want From Me?

Sometimes just having good manners can make a big difference in your relationship with your parents. Here are a few simple examples that will not only show your parents respect, but will make them feel proud of you as well.

Manners to Use with Parents

- ♥ Don't "talk back" to your parents.
- ♥ Help around the house.
- ♥ Accept the rules your parents give you.
- ♥ Always check with your parents before inviting someone over.
- ♥ Your parents need privacy sometimes—respect it.
- ♥ Having good table manners is also a way of showing respect for your parents and your family.

Table Manners You Should Know

- ♥ Come to the table with clean hands and a pleasant attitude.
- ♥ Don't begin eating until everyone has been served, or until you're asked to begin.
- ♥ Put your napkin in your lap as soon as you sit down, and keep it there throughout the meal.
- ♥ Never complain about the food. If you don't like it, don't eat it. If something is especially good, however, feel free to offer a compliment.
- ♥ Ask for things to be passed to you. Don't reach across the table.
- ♥ Chew with your mouth closed.
- ♥ Don't talk with food in your mouth.
- ♥ Keep your elbows off the table and your feet on the floor while you eat.
- ♥ Don't interrupt others while they're talking. Wait until they're finished before adding what

you have to say.

♥   Don't slump or lean back in your chair. Sit up reasonably straight, and keep all the legs of your chair on the floor.

♥   Never throw food, or anything else. This is very rude.

♥   Ask to be excused before leaving the table.

♥   Use these table manners both at home and in public.

Why Do My Parents Make So Many Crazy Rules?

Most parents have specific rules and regulations they expect you to follow while you're living with them. You may be asked to have your bed made every day and your clothes hung up. Your job may be to take out the trash each week and help put away the groceries.

Rules give you guidelines to follow. They help you decide what's right and wrong. They help you learn how to make sensible decisions so when you are older you will be able to do the same on your own.

Most parents are very clear about their rules. They also let you know what consequences will be used if you disobey those rules. When parents either don't set rules or they give you guidelines that are confusing, you need to talk with them about it. It can be very frustrating when you're later punished for something you didn't know you weren't allowed to do.

Sometimes parents are unsure of how strict the rules should be. They may not know what most parents expect or you may be the oldest child and the first one they've set rules for.

If you think they are being too strict or unfair, you need to talk with them about it. Be a good listener. There may be a good reason for the rule being as strict as it is—safety or health reasons, for example. If they don't change, at least you tried. Wait a few months and talk with them about it again. Do this honestly and politely.

You may even give your parents the idea of asking your school principal, teacher, or someone at your church for suggestions about rules. If all else fails, ask to talk to your teacher, or school social worker, or a neighbor or friend. They may have some advice that could help you.

If talking with your parent or guardian didn't solve the problem, you may want to try the following exercise.

Putting your concerns in writing can sometimes help you understand them better. The following chart may help you find a solution to your problem. Do this with the person you're having the conflict with or do it alone. You can use the chart for any problem you have at home or at school, so write the information in a spiral notebook. If you ever have a concern like it again, you'll have a solution you can consider.

Problem Solving Chart

The problem is:

_____

_____

My opinion:

_____

_____

My parents' opinion:

_____

_____

Our solution:

_____

_____

_____

Your parent may or may not discuss the problem-solving chart with you. If not, you might show it to a teacher or another trusted adult or friend and discuss it. This will help you learn from the problem. If that doesn't work, at least you tried.

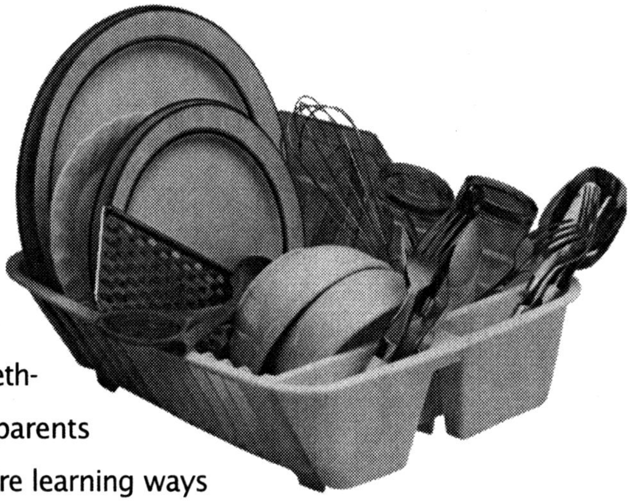

Why Are My Parents Always Making Me Feel Like A Slave By Bugging Me To Do Stuff?

It's very normal to feel that parents bug you at times. They may tell you to clean your room, feed the dog, or unload the dishwasher. Parents don't like bugging their children, but it's only fair that everyone who lives in a house together should pitch in with chores. If you don't help out, your parents will naturally be frustrated and get cranky. Remember: You're learning ways to take care of yourself when you become an adult. Your parents are trying to teach you how to be responsible. They are showing you how to take care of yourself so you will know these skills when you are an adult and on your own.

My Parents Fight A Lot. What Should I Do?

Many kids are concerned when their parents fight. Don't feel alone. It doesn't mean they don't want to be friends with each other or that they don't love each other. It could mean your parents are tense or worried. Sometimes they're just under a lot of pressure and, although they don't mean to, they get short-tempered.

It's hard to hear your parents fighting. It's also difficult to ask your parents why they're fighting. We sometimes think they might get a divorce or that someone could get hurt. Try to keep in mind that they're human and, just like other people, they don't always get along.

If you are really concerned that their fighting seems to be getting worse, you may want to tell them you're worried or scared and that you need to know what's wrong. If the fighting gets worse you need to tell someone you can trust—your teacher or school social worker. Having a hobby or activity away from your parents will help you feel less tense when they fight.

What Do I Do When I'm Home Alone And Get Really Lonely?

More and more, both parents are working outside the home in order to pay the bills or further their careers. It's quite different from years ago when most moms stayed home during the day and dads went to work. You may have to fix your own meals, entertain yourself, and yes, feel lonely. Remember your parents may not be any happier about this arrangement than you are.

Share your feelings with your parents, but try not to be upset or mad when they come home from work tired. Try to understand and talk with them about how you feel. You'll be surprised how open and understanding they'll be when you share your loneliness. Ask them if they think you're doing a good job taking care of things while they are gone. Tell them a compliment or two would give you support. It may help to talk with other kids who have to stay home alone at times. They may have suggestions for you. If you have a computer you can talk with other people and exchange ideas about hobbies, school, and sports.

Don't ever think it's your fault that your mom is working outside the home. It's not. These days, two incomes are often required to support a family comfortably. Many parents enjoy their careers, too. They may want to continue working because it adds fulfillment to their personal lives. This may help them enjoy parenthood because they don't have to choose between the two. They can do both.

Why Do My Parents Always Judge
The Friends I Hang Out With?

Your parents may decide what kinds of friends they believe you should have. It's sometimes very hard to accept the fact that when they do this, they are trying to look out for you and protect you. They feel capable of judging which friends are right for you. Don't be angry with them. Try to understand their feelings and ask to talk with them about it. Find out specifically what it is they don't like about your friend or friends. Once again, it's important that you listen. They may see some things that you're not aware of. And, they are older and more experienced with relationships.

Invite your friend over for dinner or just to spend time with you and your family. (Get your parents' permission first.) When they get to know your friend better, perhaps they'll form a different opinion. If this doesn't help after some time has passed, you'll have to make a decision to continue the friendship or end it. It's best to respect the decision your parents make, so you can maintain an honest and trusting relationship.

I'd Like To Tell My Parents I Love Them, But It's Not Easy For Me.

There are times when you feel so much love for your parents but you find it difficult to tell them or show it. Even if you've had terrible fights or run away from home once, there are always times that you feel love for your parents.

Sharing these feelings is important because it brings you and your parents closer together. It also involves communication, which is so very important in relationships.

Some kids feel their parents love them because they provide for them financially and physically. Their parents never tell them they love them, but yes, this is a way of showing love.

You can do the same. It's not necessary to say "I love you" to your parents if you care for them, but there are ways you can show it. You'd be surprised how much it will mean to them. Try some of these things sometime soon.

1. Volunteer to run an errand.
2. Before you go off by yourselves when friends come over, chat with Mom and Dad for awhile.
3. Write them a love note.
4. Offer to cook or help cook.
5. Make them a homemade item or dessert.
6. Ask to just talk.

7. Find a picture of them and put it in a frame.

8. Ask if you can go for a walk with them.

9. Have your parents show you pictures of them when they were children.

10. Clean your room.

11. Put a photo album together with their help.

12. Ask them for advice.

13. Remember their birthdays.

14. Help clean-up the car.

15. Set the table.

16. Make them breakfast in bed.

17. Take out the trash.

18. Ask them to play a game with you.

19. Give them a foot massage.

My Parents Expect More From Me Than I'm Capable Of Doing.

Some parents don't realize it, but they sometimes put pressure on children and expect too much from them. They may expect you to get straight A's in school when you are doing the best you can by getting B's. They hoped you would make the soccer team, but you never liked soccer. They may even have a college in mind for you to attend someday.

If this happens and you feel like you're under too much unnecessary pressure, you should try and talk with them about it. Maybe they don't realize how hard it is on you when you know you can't or don't want to do what they're planning for you. Discuss the things you believe you are good at. Ask them to help you make plans that revolve around your strengths, talents, and interests.

One young girl asked her former teacher to talk with her parents. After this teacher visited with them, they decided to change their plans for their daughter, because doing so would be better for her and perhaps help her become more successful. This is worth a try in some situations.

Nontraditional Families Or Extended Families (stepfamilies, single parents, foster homes)

Today, the "traditional" family of Mom, Dad, and the kids living in one house is becoming less common. Many kids do not grow up in a home with both their mother and father. They live with one or the other parent, sometimes with another relative, or in a foster home.

When parents find that they can no longer live together, they separate or get a divorce. Many lives are affected by this. Sometimes parents don't even want to get a divorce, but they realize it's the only way they will be happy.

When this happens you experience a lot of mixed emotions. Anger, fear, guilt, sadness, and disappointment are just a few— you may feel all these emotions or maybe just a few.

After the divorce, you will probably live with either your mother or father most of the time. You may also see some changes in them. They may start dating again, which can cause you to become resentful. It may be difficult for you to accept these changes. You may have felt safe and secure with the way things were and now you're uncomfortable with this new arrangement.

The divorce may not bother you in some ways, and yet it does bother you in others. It all depends on the reason for the break-up. If you lived in a situation where there was yelling and your parents were acting hateful or living like strangers, the divorce or separation may be good.

Later, you might end up living with a stepmother or stepfather who has children, too. In this situation, jealousy can create tension, but try not to let tension come between you and your new stepbrothers and stepsisters. They once went through the same thing you did. It would be great if you could stick together and support each other as much as possible.

You must understand that the divorce is not your fault. You didn't cause it, and you can't bring your parents back together. You will always be loved by your parents even though some kids feel like their parents are divorcing them, too. They're not.

Some divorces are friendly. Both parents actually get along better once they're apart. This is much easier for their children. Other divorces end in blame and anger and parents say awful things about each other. If this happens, you should never take sides. It's important that you let your parents know that you love them both, even if they dislike each other.

What Can You Do When There Is A Divorce?

♥ Many other children of divorced parents adjust very well—maybe you can talk with someone you know who has gone through it.

♥ Talking with your parents about your feelings and listening to theirs can be comforting.

♥ Try to learn something from your experience. You may be married someday and faced with some of the same problems as your parents were.

♥ Talk with your teacher, minister, or school social worker if you are extremely depressed and don't know how to handle it. You may need to talk with a counselor.

Remember:

♥ You might enjoy being around your Mom or Dad more because they're not fighting any longer.

♥ Once again, their divorce is not your fault and you can't fix it.

What Is A Foster Home?

Every so often you hear about a child who lives in a foster home, a place where children live when they are taken away from their parents. They may have been physically and mentally abused, or their parents couldn't take care of them.

Foster parents allow other children to live with them when the kids can't live in their own home. These children live with them for a few months or even as long as several years. They then go back to their first home when their parents are ready to take them.

When you live in a foster home you must follow the rules your foster parents give you. They are your parents until you leave their home.

Having to leave parents is very difficult for many kids. They feel a great loss and a lot of guilt. If this happens, you must not feel as if it's your fault. Sometimes parents need a break from the responsibility of raising children in order to straighten out their own problems.

Most of the time, you can talk with your foster parents like you would if they were your real parents. If they didn't care, you wouldn't be staying in their home to begin with. It may also be possible for you to set up a time when you can visit with your parents.

You can also ask your foster parents if they know of other kids who are in the same situation and if you could visit with them. And, if it's still very difficult for you to accept, ask your foster parents if you could talk with a doctor or counselor.

Feeling Uncomfortable Around Others

It can be very scary when the adult you are living with and trust becomes abusive. They may be your foster parents or your natural parents. They may get angry and say awful things to you or even hurt you physically. They may even pressure you into performing sexual acts with them. The abusive adult has what is called a "sickness."

You can ask the person to stop but it may not happen. The only thing you can do is tell someone. It should be a teacher, minister, rabbi, relative, or another adult you trust. Telling someone may be very hard. They may think you're exaggerating or they may not believe you at all. If the abuser is someone close to you, there may even be feelings of guilt when sharing your situation. This is normal.

You need to understand that you have the right to speak up and protect yourself. Remember to be truthful and honest about your situation. The person you tell can help you. The abuser can also be helped with trained counselors, friends, or through their church.

If you can't get help, look in the back of this book for places you can call.

When One Parent Dies

Some kids lose a parent through death. They feel angry and sad and think life has been unfair to them for taking their parent away, and it may take a long time to accept the reality of what happened. Not only do you have to adjust to the death, but also to living with a single parent.

You need to be as strong as you can. Your other parent needs you just as much as you need him or her. You've both been through a lot. This is one time when communication is extremely important.

Allow yourself to share your feelings with your other parent. It's normal to feel bad (which we call "grief") for quite a while. It takes longer for some kids to bounce back. It's also okay to talk about your other parent even if he or she is no longer around. Remember the good times you had together. Reading the chapter on Death in this book may also help.

You may have friends you can talk with. Good friends can be a wonderful support group for you at this time. Some kids feel more grown-up and responsible when a parent dies. They realize that they have to pitch in more and take on more chores. This can help you feel proud of yourself. Some parents and kids find special things to do together to become closer.

If you or your family are having a hard time adjusting, you may need counseling to help you get through your sadness. This is nothing to be embarrassed about, and it shows that you are taking control of your actions and liking yourself enough to want to get better.

Working through problems with your family is sometimes difficult. But you must try—for yourself. If you've done everything possible, then move on and know that you should concentrate on creating a happy life for yourself some other way.

Notes

CHAPTER

4

Siblings

Our families. What do we do with them and what would we do without them? Growing up in a family can be one of the most exciting and heartwarming experiences. The love you share with your brother or sister can be very special. The emotions you experience are memories you'll have for a lifetime. The bond of trust and love will last throughout your adult years.

On the other hand, being related doesn't necessarily mean you'll always share close family feelings. Life just isn't that way. Conflicts between you and a brother or sister are very natural. Some kids experience anger and loneliness in their family. There may be yelling, jealousy, and put-downs. Some of this occurred in my own family. With nine brothers and sisters, there were bound to be problems at one time or another.

Fighting amongst brothers and sisters seems to occur in almost every home at one time or another. When kids have problems relating, they fight with each other. It's their way of communicating their concerns. Since they aren't adults yet, they don't have the skills for working out problems, so they fight.

Parents or guardians then step in, not to take sides, but to make decisions and resolve differences.

What Causes Siblings To Fight?

1.   One may have a larger bedroom. Or, some homes do not have enough bedrooms for everyone, so they share. If this concerns you, talk with your parents about it. Maybe you could change bedrooms now and then and later you'll get your turn to have the larger one.

2.   Your brother or sister may have more friends. You may spend a lot of your time by yourself or with just one friend. Making friends may be harder for you. Ask your other friend and older sister if they could introduce you to some new people.

3.   One or the other of you might get higher grades. Getting C's and B's is probably the best you can do. If this is causing problems, it's best to discuss it with one or both parents. Ask them if you could do something special when you bring home a good test grade. Not necessarily an A, but a grade you earned for doing your best. This also means your parents should see you studying for this test.

4.   Your brother may be more athletic. Your family may get recognition because he's a football star. They may never (or very seldom) compliment you for what you do well. It's time to visit with your parents and maybe even your athletic brother. Let them know how you feel. Don't get angry or blame them for anything. They may not even know they are causing you to feel this way. You'd be surprised how understanding families can be when everyone talks about the problem together. Many jealousies build and become worse because of lack of communication.

5.   Someone in the family may get more privileges. Some kids think older siblings are allowed to

do more. Others may get more attention and cuddling because they are younger. It's important to understand that parents don't necessarily give the same privileges to all kids in the family. If you think they are being unfair, talk with them about it. You may find out that they are being more fair than you realize.

6.   Sometimes kids fight just to fight. It could be that they are angry at someone else or like getting on someone's nerves for fun. They may even have a lot of time on their hands and nothing else to do. You might want to start a new hobby or activity if you have a great deal of free time. Not only will this prevent you from becoming annoyed with your brother or sister, but it may help you feel less grumpy.

Working out your differences while you're growing up is very important. If you don't, it can lead to hatred and resentment in later years. It's possible that it can affect your own children someday. They may never have the chance to meet their cousins because you and your family member aren't speaking. They could even grow up disliking their cousins because they saw the resentment you had toward your siblings.

How Can I Solve Problems With My Brothers And Sisters?

Ask your parents to have a family discussion. Everyone meets to express concerns that are bothering them or questions they may have. It should not be a get-together for blaming anyone, but to express opinions about situations they are unhappy with. You may have to be the one to schedule the meeting. If the whole family won't come, discuss your concerns with those who do show up. You can then talk about solutions and try to come to an agreement.

Remember to use good manners:

- ♥ No yelling.
- ♥ No blaming and accusing.
- ♥ Use appropriate language (no swearing).
- ♥ Be a good listener.
- ♥ Respect the other person's feelings.
- ♥ Don't leave the meeting angry.
- ♥ No arguing allowed.
- ♥ Take turns speaking.

These skills will serve you well in the future when you are an adult.

If you still feel some anger even though you've had the family discussion, there are several things you can do:

1. Take a long walk and talk to yourself about your anger as if someone were listening. If your dog goes along, talk to him.

2. Kick rocks, punch your pillow, or yell at the trees.

3. Ride your bike or talk with a friend.

4. Write it down. Describe all of your angry feelings like you were talking with someone. After that throw the paper away. Better yet, flush it down the toilet. Let your anger go far, far away.

If you feel a lot of frustration because of your family, it is important to talk with someone who can listen and give good suggestions. You do not have to deal with it alone. You can talk with a relative, minister or rabbi, social worker, teacher, or someone else you trust. And, remember, don't blame yourself if things at home aren't going well. Some of us just aren't very lucky with families.

There are times when a sister or brother cannot get along, no matter what. It may be because of jealousy or lack of problem-solving skills. Whatever the reason, if nothing brings them together they may be strangers or enemies for a long time.

When this happens you need to remember how hard you tried to form a good relationship with the sibling. Don't blame yourself if you've done everything you can to resolve your differences. Even if your brother or sister won't speak to you, at least you know you've given your all and that will help you keep peace with yourself.

What If I'm An Only Child?

Being an only child can make you feel very special. You don't have to put up with brothers or sisters bugging you. You have your own bedroom and there is plenty of room when someone spends the night.

Not having a brother or sister can also cause some loneliness. At times you may wish there were other youngsters around. I know of kids who wish they had siblings, and others who would give their

brothers or sisters away in a minute.

If you are an only child, you can have friends over, do things with other kids, or spend time with friends who have brothers and sisters.

Another way to occupy yourself is with a pen pal. You can get names of kids who wish to be pen pals from your teacher. I know girls who have several pen pals all over the world.

The computer is another way you can entertain yourself. As I mentioned earlier, you can talk with people from all over the world on the computer, not to mention the growing number of computer programs available for kids today.

You can't control the number of siblings in your family, but you can talk with your parents about it, or find other friends and interests to occupy your time while interacting with others.

My Sister Is Disabled

Having a disabled family member can cause sadness as well as joy. You may have a sister who is paralyzed from the waist down or a brother with one arm.

It's sometimes difficult for individuals outside and within your family to understand and accept a person who is disabled. Our society puts much emphasis on having a "perfect body," "perfect teeth," a "perfect personality," and a "perfect life." This attitude is slowly changing. Parking lots, bathrooms, and many other public areas are continuing to provide services for the handicapped.

I believe we are all disabled in one way and we are all talented or gifted in another. For example:

- A superstar basketball player may have to use orthotics in his athletic shoes because his feet cannot support his body.
- A young girl in a wheelchair sells hundreds of watercolor paintings on greeting cards which she painted by holding a paintbrush in her mouth.
- Your father may be a super carpenter, but can't bend his knee because of an injury.
- Your teacher has won national honors, but she can't swim and she can never have a child by natural childbirth.
- The state award winning soccer coach has a glass eye.

You see, if you really think about people you'll discover that there are many with disabilities. We just seem to notice it more when it's physical. Too many times we focus on the disability instead of the personality, not realizing what a handicapped person is capable of doing.

Our parents may give the disabled sister more attention. This is because they're concerned and must take care of her. If you see them becoming overprotective, try to talk with them about it. It may be that they aren't realizing it. Try arranging a time when you can do something special alone with your parents.

I'll always remember a grandfather in our community who was raising his grandson (who was in a wheelchair), because the boy's parents didn't want him. The grandfather took him to basketball games, the park, movie theater, and to church. He was a wonderful example for our community. He demonstrated compassion, concern, care, and loyalty for another human being. He is seen by many others as a hero. I'm sure that one day his grandson will try and do the same for someone else.

How you see and treat a disabled person is a state of mind. If you tell yourself they're different and strange, chances are you'll believe it and those negative messages will show. On the other hand, if you accept the person with her disabilities, you will feel easier about being around her. Think how much joy you will give to the disabled person for showing you understand and care.

Notes

CHAPTER 5

FRIENDS

What is a friend? Your friends are the people who like being around you because of who you are. They are people you can trust, and who care about you. They give you advice to help you, not to hurt you. Friends listen when you need someone to talk to. Sometimes they even help you solve your problems. You feel warm and special when you're with good friends.

How Do I Choose A Friend?

Choosing a friend is easier some days than others. It also depends on where you are and how many kids you're around.

Each year, I watch my students make friends with each other. Students who are shy and like being alone have a more difficult time than kids who like being involved with others. Don't think being by yourself a lot means you can't make friends. It's just that in order to form a friendship, you must make an effort to do so. Talking or communicating is necessary in order for that to happen. If you're not very good at it, there are ways you can learn. Read on.

When Making Friends, Consider The Following:

1. Watch other kids and see how they act. Do they treat others with respect or do they bully them and make negative comments in hurtful ways? Do they share and allow others to have recognition, or are they one-sided and selfish?

The reason this is so important is because how you see that person treat others is probably the way he or she will treat you. Sharing, respect, and trust are just a few good qualities you look for in a good friend. If you're not treated the way you feel you deserve to be treated by the other person, the friendship will never work.

2. In addition to this, you should watch what other kids are interested in. If you participate in soccer or other sports, you would want a friend who is also interested in these activities. If your favorite pastime is biking, try to meet someone who also likes riding bikes.

3. Don't make friends with someone with whom you have nothing in common. But, just because you are in the same class or in the same group activity doesn't mean you'd be good for each other. Be careful how you choose your new friend. It's better to be sure than sorry. Undoing the friendship could be difficult and very painful. You may have to deal with bad experiences in relationships as you grow older. Don't add to them by entering into an unworkable friendship and then having to end it.

4. Lastly, don't ever let people pressure you into a friendship. I remember when a new girl, "Tina," in junior high (who always wore nice clothes) was asked to be friends with another classmate. Let's call her "Nancy." When Tina became friends with Nancy, she started asking Tina if she could borrow her clothes. She said, "If you let me borrow your sweater, I'll be your friend forever." Tina didn't have any friends so she let Nancy borrow her sweater and a lot of other things, including money. Nancy took advantage of Tina so badly that Tina's parents had to put a stop to it. Nancy was mad and started rumors around school about Tina and many kids believed them because they didn't know her very well.

So, you can see how important it is to select good friends who respect you for the person you are instead of for the wrong reasons.

You probably just read the chapters, "Feeling Good About Yourself" and "Assertiveness." Read them again before you start making your new friend. You must believe that you are a worthy person who deserves respect from others and is allowed to express your true feelings. Don't ever feel you're less important than the person whom you're making friends with. Stand up to what you believe in and don't let others persuade you to act in a way that causes you to feel uncomfortable.

Where Can I Meet Friends?

School is only one place to meet friends. You can meet new kids while you're participating in community activities like gymnastics, soccer, musical events, special interest classes, or religious functions. If your mom or dad belongs to an organization, you may be able to meet friends through your parents, who know other families. You could even ask other friends to introduce you to some of their friends. Your teachers might suggest kids who would be good for you.

You now know the many different places where friendships can be formed. However, remember you must be careful who you choose to be your friend. Also, having many friends, who aren't necessarily good friends, is not as important as having one or two who you can trust.

What If I Don't Belong To A Group?

How Can I Find A Person Who Would Make A Good Friend?

First of all, decide on an interest. Fill out the questionnaire below.

Yes or No

_____	Likes being alone.
_____	Likes being with others.
_____	Is involved with sports.
_____	Spends a lot of time with family.
_____	Likes going places.
_____	Likes listening to others.
_____	Enjoys working on projects.
_____	Likes to read.
_____	Likes going to movies.
_____	Likes talking on the phone.
_____	Likes doing volunteer work.
_____	Enjoys being involved in school activities.

After you have answered yes or no to the exercise above, try and think of one to three kids you're around who may have the same interests. Remember: you have to watch and listen in order to learn about the people around you. And, go back and read the four steps on "When Making New Friends" before you begin.

Another good idea would be to become involved in an activity that interests you. Look on your questionnaire. If you like to read, ask a friend to go to the library with you and look for new books. After you've read them, you could then go for ice cream and discuss the books.

If you like working on projects, ask your teacher if there is a committee in school you could sign up for. Or ask your minister or rabbi if there is a youth group you could join.

There are people all around you who can help you meet new people. If you still are not sure how to do this, ask your teacher, school social worker, clergyperson, or parents. It is not impossible to make friends.

Friends, what is a friend, when to make friends.

How Do I Start?

If you're shy, it may be a little harder for you to meet new kids. A couple of ways to do this are:

1. Introduce yourself to someone you don't know by saying, "Hi, I noticed you're new at this school. My name is _____. Is there anything I can tell you about the school or the teachers?"

2. "Hi, I noticed you're new in this school. Would you like to eat lunch together, or get together this weekend? I have this great CD we could listen to."

I'm sure you can think of many other things to say when meeting someone for the first time.

Remember: If someone turns you down, try again with someone else. Don't let rejection stop you. I believe that if other kids don't take an interest in you, then the friendships were never meant to be. It's their loss. Who knows, you may meet up again someday and form a friendship then. I've known this to happen many times.

Peer Pressure

I have asked some of my pre-teen students what they felt were the greatest pressures amongst teens today. The answers? Peer pressure, drugs, smoking, alcohol, and cliques. They said they experience constant pressure because of at least one of these issues. They feel pressured to do what someone else wants instead of their friends accepting the choices they make.

A mistake some kids make is giving in to peer pressure (pressure from kids your own age to do something you don't want to). They don't value themselves or have much respect for who they are. They think other kids will like them if they do what they're told. The truth is, other kids won't. Kids putting on the pressure will only bully and control you if you allow it. It's like the story I told you about Tina and the sweater. Tina's friend liked her as long as Tina let her use her personal items. Once the friend couldn't control Tina, she no longer cared for her.

True friends do not act this way or pressure you. They also don't need to control you because they like who they are.

If you remember to practice your skills about learning how to be self-confident and how to be assertive, the challenge of peer pressure can help you feel proud of yourself for standing up for your beliefs.

Why Is There Pressure To Take Drugs And Alcohol?

Some reasons you may be pressured into drugs and/or alcohol include:

1. Everyone else you're around may be doing it.

2. Your friends are already hooked on it. They think if you use drugs or alcohol, then it makes it more acceptable for them.

3. Some kids think it will help your problems go away, when all it does is add to your problems.

4. It may be easy to get ahold of.

If you decide to give in to peer pressure, you must realize that you will have to live with the consequences. The person pressuring you has nothing to lose. You're the one who cannot turn back and change that "first step" once the decision is made.

I will discuss more about this in the Drugs chapter.

Pressure To Smoke

The pressure to smoke may not seem very serious to you, especially since cigarettes are sold over the counter. Tobacco advertising also tries to convince you that cigarettes will improve your life or you will be happier if you smoke.

One of the best things you can do when deciding whether or not to smoke, is to talk with someone who has quit. It may be someone who had to quit because they had serious health problems or for other reasons, too. The advice you receive may give you the support you need if you're being pressured to smoke. The same is true for drugs and alcohol.

Pressure To Skip Classes

At one time or another, the group you hang out with may try to talk you into skipping classes. They may ask you to skip because they need someone to hang out with. Maybe their grades aren't as good as yours and they know that skipping could cause your grades to fall. (Of course they won't admit this.)

Once again, you must consider the consequences when making a decision you are not comfortable with. How will skipping classes affect your grades? What will you tell your parents when you get caught? Will you be suspended from school? How will it affect your reputation with teachers at school? These are serious questions to ask yourself. If you really think this through, peer pressure isn't as bad as what you will have to live with later on.

Pressure To Join A Clique Or A Group

A clique is somewhat like a club except for one thing. A clique is a group that pressures or forces you into doing things you are uneasy about. They are kids who try to make you feel guilty if you don't do and say what they want you to.

Being asked to join a clique can be flattering. You feel accepted and secure. However, belonging to a clique can make you feel overwhelmed. The pressure to do everything may become too much. Like I said at the beginning of this book, joining a clique can cause you to lose control of your own decisions. You may be pressured into doing things you may not be comfortable with.

Be very careful if deciding to join a clique. Once you belong to the group it will be very difficult to get out. If the clique starts moving toward drugs or sex, you may then want to leave. You may need help from a friend to do this. Getting involved in after-school clubs or group activities can keep you busy so that you have something to do when the clique gets together. Leave the group gradually. Hang out with them less and less. You can also have your parents help by asking them not to let you go when the group calls.

Your friends in the clique may not like you moving out of their circle, but moving away gradually is better than getting angry with each other. After all, you may have to face them at school. Just continue to say "hi" when you see them and walk on by.

So once again you see the consequences of joining a clique. Is all this trouble really worth it? Take some time to think about it. You may even talk with a person who has been in a clique and has left.

Making The Right Decision

It's sometimes easy to let others make decisions for you. Especially if you made a bad decision once or twice and are afraid you will do it again. Remember the "assertiveness" chapter? I told you that learning to be assertive takes practice. Well, it's that same way when you're learning how to make choices. It takes practice, too. In order to do this, you must practice making decisions based on your beliefs and values and what makes you feel comfortable—not what someone else wants.

Others may try to convince you that your decision is wrong because they don't agree with it. This is when you need to be strong and politely stick with what you're comfortable with and not give in.

There is a difference between compromising and letting someone control your decision or peer pressure. When people compromise, they agree to one decision that everyone can accept. You don't get everything your own way. Each person takes part in the decision in order to come to an agreement. No one person controls the other and all opinions are respected. This is a healthy and productive way of communicating.

Peer pressure, on the other hand, is when you're forced or pressured into making a decision that others want. They may even bully you or threaten you if you don't do what they ask. This is very wrong and unhealthy.

What Do I Do If I Can't Handle The Peer Pressure?

If you're in a situation where the peer pressure is too much for you to handle, it's time to get help. Probably the best place to go is to your parents. I know this may be difficult, especially if you're not used to talking with them. You may even be living with one parent who has many problems and seems too overwhelmed to hear about yours. Use your best judgement.

Try telling your parents what's happened. If doing that doesn't help, then go elsewhere. It doesn't mean your parents don't love you or understand your problems. It may be that they don't know what to do. Thank them for listening and being there for you.

You can ask to talk with a school counselor, social worker, teacher, or someone at your church or temple. A friend's mother or neighbor can also help you if she's someone you trust. Keep asking until someone can help you. You don't have to handle your problems by yourself. Once again, don't feel embarrassed to ask for help. Most people do at one time or another.

What Can I Do When My Friend And I Aren't Getting Along?

Relationships aren't always easy. You may argue over clothes, how you spend your free time, boys, and other friends. Disagreeing from time to time is just part of human nature. No one gets along all of the time.

If you and your friend are fighting, try as much as possible to work it out if you think the friendship is worth saving. It may be that you're arguing over something you think is bad for you—drugs, smoking, skipping school, etc. Then it's time for you to let your friend know how you feel and ask her to accept your feelings. Tell her you aren't comfortable with going along with what she's asking you to do and that you hope she understands.

Some ways you can do this are:

- ♥ I hope you understand what I'm going to say…
- ♥ You know how I feel right now?…
- ♥ Put yourself in my place…
- ♥ I don't feel comfortable with this because…
- ♥ I know we're both really upset right now…
- ♥ How do you think we can both work to solve this?…

Remember to express your feelings honestly. Don't make excuses for the way you feel. Don't raise your voice or blame anyone while discussing your fight. Express your feelings, but also be a good listener.

Some kids find that a few days away from each other after the talk gives them a chance to think about the fight. But don't stop talking for too long. You don't want it to grow worse than it is. The sooner you can solve the problem and make amends, the better.

If talking with your friend doesn't solve anything, try asking your parents, teacher, or another adult friend you can trust for advice. If this doesn't help, then it may be best to go your separate ways. You can do this politely. Who knows, you may be friends again someday.

My Friend And I Aren't As Close As We Used To Be.

I remember when my daughter and her friend slowly discovered other kids they liked being with. They eventually started to quarrel over the silliest things. I noticed how each one felt a little guilty when they spent time with other friends. They were used to doing everything together all of the time, but suddenly found the need to explore other friendships.

Relationships change as people get older. It may be because of different interests, meeting new kids in school, or moving from one end of town to another. It doesn't mean you can't be friends any longer. It just means your interests are changing.

There is no reason why you can't continue to see your old friend while meeting new ones. It's actually better to do things with other people once in awhile. Otherwise, when your friend goes some-where or can't be with you, you will have to find ways to occupy your time by yourself. You may not like doing this if it happens frequently.

You and your friend may want to read this chapter together. It may help you understand how friendships are bonded through trust and respect for each other's feelings and needs. It would be great for both of you to know that you still care for each other, but you just don't want to hang around each other as often.

How Do I Keep Friends?

Keeping friends takes some effort. It means asking them to do things instead of always expecting them to call you. It also means being with them when they're not in their best mood. When things aren't going well between the two of you, good friends make an effort to mend broken relationships.

The following suggestions may help you keep the good friends you already have and possibly make new ones.

- ♥ Always be truthful and honest (but positive) when communicating.
- ♥ Accept your friend even if she's different from you.
- ♥ Allow the other person to develop other friendships.
- ♥ Accept the other person's opinion, even if it's different from yours.
- ♥ Be willing to compromise and negotiate when you disagree.
- ♥ Use good manners around your friends.

A good friend is like a special seashell you find near the ocean, one that sparkles on the outside and has unique rings swirling within—rings and ridges you want to know more about. That good friend sparkles too. She listens and shares her rings of understanding, suggestions, and concerns when you're trying to float in the ocean of this mysterious world. Like that seashell, a good friend is unique and should be saved and cherished forever.

Notes

Notes

Dealing With Death

People die at different ages and for different reasons. They may be sick with an illness or killed in an automobile accident; they may die from a heart attack, suicide, or just old age.

No matter what caused the death, losing someone you know may be very difficult to accept. The loss may be overwhelming, especially if it was someone close to you.

Some of my past students have shared experiences with me about a friend, sibling, or relative who had died. They each had expressed feelings of death differently. Some shared memories of happiness; others cried while talking about it. Some reminisced about a death when our classroom pet died. There are even signs of grief when we read about the death of a character in a book.

It's normal for kids to feel angry and confused about death. There are always questions about why the death occurred, and they may even blame themselves or someone else for the death.

When a close friend dies, especially without warning, it can cause unbelievable shock and pain. How severe that pain is depends on how close you were and how much time you spent together.

If you spent a lot of time together, you may feel a very deep loneliness along with depression.

Not having your friend around will take some getting used to. There will be some suffering until you adjust.

At first you might feel shock and disbelief. As days pass, you may begin to accept the loss—especially when you don't see that person any more.

Talking with your friend's parents, relatives, or someone close to them can be helpful. Having a close support person, whether it is a relative or someone else, can also be extremely beneficial.

When an older person dies because of health problems or old age, we seem to accept it more easily. They've lived a long life and the suffering they experienced was hard on them. This is also the case when a younger person is expected to die. Friends and family suffer a great deal just watching the dying person hang on to the last breath of life. The dying person may even be attached to tubes or machines that keep him or her alive. This is painful for families to watch. They would rather have their loved one die with dignity and respect than be kept alive only to exist in a hospital bed, unable to breathe without machines, knowing that death is near.

If this is happening with someone in your family, it would help to talk with your parents, doctor, or a friend about your feelings. Don't feel badly if you need to cry.

Recently a father of two died of cancer. It was very hard for his children. When they visited him, they saw so much pain on his face. The mother cut down on the number of visits the kids made to their dying father because it was so painful for them to see him suffer. When they did visit, the father made taped conversations with his children so they would have memories of him after he died. What a beautiful gift from a dying parent. Good memories of the person you've lost are very important.

Another difficult situation is when a loved one of a friend dies; it's hard to find the right words to say or know how to act. You may even feel pressured to come up with ways to get her through her grief. Don't. Your friend doesn't expect that from you. Tell her how sorry you are and that you would like to be there for her if she needs to talk or wants to do things with you. Let her know that you understand, be there for her, even if she doesn't have much to say. Allow her to feel her emotions and be a good listener. Just be yourself. Isn't that what you would want?

Other times a death is caused by suicide, when someone takes her or his own life. Not long ago, my daughter came home from junior high school in tears because a classmate of hers tried to take her own life. I will never forget how affected she and her friends were when it happened. Suicide can be very confusing and you may never know why someone would want to die.

If you ever hear someone say she feels like killing herself, and she sounds serious, you need to tell someone. Tell a teacher or your parents. Consider this is a call for help. Something is causing her to be depressed and unhappy. Some warning signs for suicide are loss of interest in activities or in normally fun things, overdoses of drugs and alcohol, slits on wrists, being alone or sad for too long, or any other unusual change in behavior.

If talking with someone she knows is uncomfortable for your friend, she can call 911 or one of the hotline numbers in the back of this book. That way she can get help and no one needs to know she called.

It's upsetting to hear of so many young people committing suicide. It's also sad that some people who commit suicide blame others. The reason may be the breakup of a relationship, losing friends, even low self-esteem. Some even leave suicide notes for people to find after they are gone. This can cause much guilt and pain for people who knew them. It is important to realize that most such problems only last for a short time and most problems can be helped, even though it may seem like the end of the world. Suicide is not a good way to solve a problem. So many suicides could be prevented if only people contacted a support person they could talk to.

You must realize that the only person responsible is the person who killed herself. You are not responsible for someone else's suicide attempt. You can talk with the person and offer support if you hear her talking about it, but you cannot take responsibility for her suicide.

Another reason some people commit suicide is because of a boyfriend/girlfriend breakup. I remember a girl once saying, "When I broke up with my boyfriend, I didn't want to live any more. I couldn't stand a day without him in my life. Now that I'm a few years older and have a new boyfriend, I think back and realize how stupid I was. My old boyfriend has a great life and I do too. I almost took away my precious life because of one unhappy moment back then. That's serious and scary." This story is a good reminder of how suicide is a permanent solution to a temporary problem.

We All Grieve Differently

We all have our own way of grieving. Some people cry for a long time; others cry only during or after the funeral—or not at all. You might even know of people who have isolated themselves from everyone for a while because they needed to grieve alone. There are also those who leave their house constantly to be with friends because they don't want to be by themselves. They may go to parties, movies, or social events to get their mind off of the death.

Anger is also a normal feeling when there is a loss. You may be angry at God, yourself, or someone else because you felt it was their fault for causing the death or that you let them down.

It's important that you express your anger in an appropriate way. You are not a bad person for feeling angry. Just don't hurt someone else with your words or actions. Take a long walk and scream at the trees. Throw rocks into a lake as far as you can. Throw all your anger into the water and let it drown. Tell someone about your angry thoughts or feelings.

Emotional pain is different for everyone. It may be so bad that you feel you can't go on another day. You may feel numb and very empty. This is nature's way of helping you deal with the loss. The numbness shelters your body from any more hurt. I have always believed that God allows us only as much pain as we can handle. It's then up to us to help heal ourselves.

This is when you need to take special care of yourself. Try to stay away from unnecessary stress. Don't try to stop your feelings. Allow your body to feel the pain. Accept how you feel, tell yourself it's okay, and never feel guilty because of those feelings.

A psychologist once told me, "Our thoughts and feelings are like little drawers inside of our heads. We pull out the drawer of thoughts we need to think about and close it up and put it back when we are finished with it. The drawer may need to be opened for a long time and it may need to be opened frequently. Other times a drawer of thoughts may only need to be opened once in a great while and not for a very long time."

When we grieve, that drawer inside of our mind may need to stay open for a long time. It may need to be opened often. But as you heal, the drawer will have to be opened less and less. Open your drawer of thoughts when you need to and put it back when you are ready. The thoughts inside your drawer will never be completely forgotten. You will just think about them less and less.

Again and again we have heard people say, "If only I would have done this, or if only I would have done that." Don't blame yourself with "what-ifs." When my sister, Anita, was killed in a car accident, we all felt bad. Especially my father. He hadn't wanted her to drive on cold, icy roads that night and had tried to stop her. She, being 19 and very independent, decided to go anyway. The car slid off the road into a ditch and she was killed.

My father said, "If only I would have stopped her. If only, if only, if only."

Sometimes awful things happen and we can't do anything

to stop it. Most of the time, no one can.

Don't ever feel like you have control when someone dies. You can't. When it's their time, it happens. Don't ever feel responsible.

How Can I Help Myself Deal With The Loss?

There are many ways you can help yourself heal.

Talk with others.

A best friend or someone who's experienced a loss can be very helpful at this time. You may ask your friends to tell you how they felt and how they helped themselves get over it. Talk about your good memories of the person you lost.

Write in a journal.

Write as if you were talking with someone. Write your feelings of anger and depression as well as the joyful things you remember about her.

Reach out to someone who needs help.

Help clean up an elderly person's yard or a teacher's room at school. Call your local community service center and ask if there is anything kids can do to help. If the death was in your family, your Mom or Dad would love it if you volunteer for a few extra chores.

Listen to music and try a new hobby.

Listening to your favorite music and doing something you enjoy can make you feel so much better. You may even ask a friend to join you. Becoming involved and focusing on the positive can help you learn to appreciate your own life.

Pray.

You can do this in church or temple or at home by yourself or with your family. Talking to God can be very soothing and peaceful and he always understands.

How Can I Help Others Deal With Loss?

I've talked about different and normal ways people deal with pain. However, if you notice some unusual behavior from a family member or friend, you may want to tell someone who can help.

…Is she taking drugs or alcohol to ease the pain?

…Is the person spending too much time alone?

…Has the person stopped eating?

…Does she talk about dying every day?

…Has she lost interest in people and events around her?

…Has she started doing poorly in school?

Watch carefully. One or more of the above is a call for help—not only for a friend, but if you experience these feelings then you should seek help. You have to think about healing and getting better. Seeking help is another way to accomplish that.

If you can't get over the loss after a reasonable amount of time, it's time for you to get professional help. Ask your parents or teacher if you can speak to a counselor or social worker. Your parents could also ask your family doctor to recommend someone.

If you prefer to do this on your own, look in the phone book under "psychologists" or "psychotherapists." Try and find one that deals with families or specializes in grief counseling. That first phone call will help you feel better right away.

Don't feel embarrassed to ask for help. It isn't any different from being physically ill. At times we need a trained specialist to help us heal when we can't do it on our own. Even though most people can get by without help, they can get through their grief more easily with help so that the loss does not cause as much disruption.

What Does Death Teach Us?

Death teaches us to appreciate what we have. It reminds us how lucky we are to wake up each morning and enjoy another day of living, when others haven't been so lucky.

I remember talking with a friend who was dying of cancer. She said she enjoyed listening to sounds which she had always taken for granted. Sounds of traffic in the morning and firewood being cut were reminders of life around her. She also started to pay more attention to the beautiful sights around her.

So you see, sometimes when we know things will be taken away, we only then realize how lucky we are to be alive to enjoy them.

We don't know the reasons why people die at a certain time. It just happens. When it does it is sometimes such a shock that it takes a long time until we feel normal again. It's like a wound you get when you hurt your arm or leg. Eventually it heals, but the scar is still there and we go on with our life.

Notes

Notes

My Changing Body

As I've said, you will eventually enter a stage called "puberty." This is when you're a teenager and your body is changing into a woman. You can tell when this happens because you start going through many physical and emotional changes.

Some noticeable changes are:

♥ Pimples appear on your face.

- ♥ You begin having periods, which may not come at the same time each month.

- ♥ You notice more and darker hair on your legs and under your arms.

- ♥ Your breasts start growing.

- ♥ Pubic hair begins to grow around your genital area.

- ♥ You feel depressed at times for no reason.

- ♥ You have sexual feelings.

- ♥ Your face tends to have more oil on it.

- ♥ Your hair needs to be washed more often.

- ♥ You'll need to wear deodorant because you will sweat more.

- ♥ Taking a bath each day is also necessary to prevent body odor.

Your thoughts and feelings about growing up will vary. Some days you will feel excited about not being a kid any more and you will like the special privileges you're allowed as you grow older. Other days you may feel embarrassed about your bodily changes and you may even feel like you're not ready to be a grownup.

These feelings are normal. They're all part of becoming an adult. Deciding how to handle this time in your life can be confusing. Reading material like this book can help, and so can talking with teachers, parents, social workers, and other adults you trust. Don't ever feel like you have to go through this time by yourself. You don't.

I believe that your mind is incredibly powerful. If you are positive about growing up, chances are this time will be an enjoyable experience for you. I hope you choose to welcome changes and celebrate becoming an adult and learn to love who you are at every stage of your life. No, it isn't always easy, but it can be done. It's up to you to decide how you choose to feel.

Remember, you're growing into a special and beautiful young woman, like a caterpillar turning into a beautiful butterfly.

You can change your negative thoughts about growing up into positive ones. Here are some examples of how growing up your ATTITUDE affects you:

	NEGATIVE	POSITIVE
1.	I'm worried that my parents will expect too much from me.	My parents give me more responsibility which improves my self-confidence.
2.	I always wake up with pimples on my face.	Thank goodness this acne is just a phase I'll be over soon!
3.	I have terrible menstrual cramps every month.	How exciting that my body is changing, so that someday I can have a baby.
4.	The boys in school make remarks about my breasts. It embarrasses me.	The boys at school make remarks about my breasts. I guess they see I'm becoming a woman.
5.	I'm taller than most other girls my age; it seems weird.	Since I'm taller and look more grownup, I will be able to get my own job.
6.	There isn't anything for teens to do in our town.	I am allowed to make my own decisions when I'm with my friends. It makes me feel important.
7.	It's a pain hanging around adults.	I like my private time when I stay home instead of always going along with my parents. I can put a puzzle together, read, play on the computer, or just relax and listen to music.
8.	No one ever listens to me.	I can talk with adults about serious and grownup information.
9.	Now that I'm allowed to date, I'm afraid no one will want to ask me to do things with him.	When I get my driver's license, I'll be able to go places on my own without bothering my parents to take me.

What kind of thoughts do you have each day? Are they positive or negative? Do you have more negative thoughts than positive? If so, try turning one negative thought into a positive one every so often. It may take a while for you to do this, and it may take practice, but it works. You'll be surprised how much better you feel when you're feeling good thoughts. There's no better way to improve your self-confidence.

Breasts

As you begin to mature, you will notice that your breasts develop. Many girls are self-conscious about this. Some of this embarrassment comes from unkind remarks boys make when they notice girls developing.

A girl's breasts are made up of soft body tissue and mammary glands. As she grows older, these glands begin to produce ducts so that, as a mature woman, she can provide milk if she has a baby.

Every girl's breasts develop at a different time, depending on the activity of the pituitary gland and when certain hormones in her body are released. The different stages may begin as early as age eight or as late as fifteen—or even later. Nothing will hurry the process.

Your breasts may feel quite sensitive, especially before your menstrual period. Some swelling may also be noticeable, but this will go away when your period is over.

Like your feet being different sizes, don't be alarmed if one of your breasts is slightly larger than the other. This is quite common.

You will also notice that there is quite a difference in breast sizes among girls. Cup sizes range anywhere from AA to DD. The size of your breasts is determined by the genes you inherit from your parents.

When do I start wearing a bra?

Many times girls want to begin wearing a bra because they see other girls their age wearing them. You and your mom should together decide when the time is right.

Determining my bra size

To determine how many inches around your chest, wrap a tape measure around your body right below your rib cage (under both breasts). Add five inches to the number on the tape measure to get the inch measurement of your bra. To determine your cup size, I recommend that you try on a bra to decide whether you are AA, A, B, C, or D. I say this because bra sizes vary, and often the only true measurement you get is when you put on a bra and feel that it's a good, comfortable fit. Most lingerie salespeople can help you select the correct bra size and style.

Bras for medium or large breasts

An underwire bra is the best choice for good support and lift.

Bras for small breasts

Wide straps are a good choice because they won't slip off your shoulders. Light padding inside the bra will help give you shape and lift.

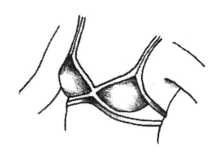

Breast examinations

It's important to examine your breasts at least once a month. This can be done easily when you're in the shower. If you find any lumps or if you feel something that seems different, ask your parents to make an appointment with your doctor for you. Your doctor will examine you more closely to make sure everything is okay.

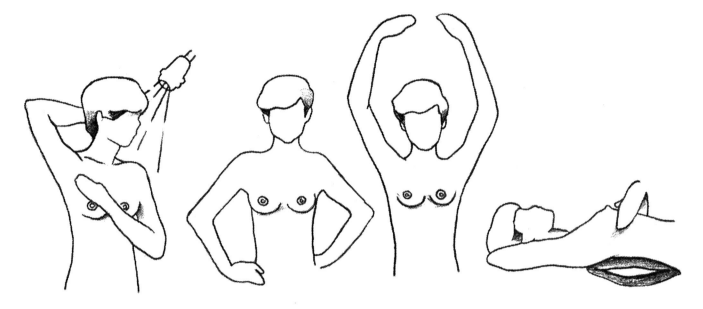

How do I examine my breasts?

1. Place your right arm behind your head. Use your left hand to feel the entire right breast. Next, place your left arm behind your head and use your right hand to feel the entire left breast. Check for lumps in each breast.

2. While standing in front of a mirror with your arms at your sides, look for any swelling or changes in your nipples.

3. While lying down with a pillow under your right shoulder, place your right hand behind your head. Using your left hand, press in circular motions all over until you reach the nipple. Squeeze the nipple gently to make sure there is no discharge; if there is, tell your parents. Then put the pillow under your left shoulder, place your left hand behind your head, and repeat the process for your left breast.

Examine your breasts a week after your period. Don't panic if you find something unusual. Most changes and breast lumps are not dangerous.

Many doctors will show you how to examine your breasts when you start developing. The age varies with each girl. If you practice checking for lumps as you go through puberty, it will give you a good idea how you should look for any abnormal changes when your breasts are fully developed.

Breasts are a very feminine part of your body. You should not feel embarrassed about them, but proud, for you are now becoming a woman.

What are "private parts"?

Your sex organs are sometimes called your "private parts." This term is a slang word people use when they want to avoid the actual words used for sexual body parts. These parts of your body are necessary for you to function as a healthy human being. Although many people have slang names for these organs, it's important that you know their right names and what they do. This will help you understand your body and be more confident and comfortable.

The internal parts are:

1. Uterus: Also called the womb, this is where a baby grows when a woman is pregnant. The uterus protects the unborn baby.

2. Cervix: Sometimes this is referred to as the neck of the uterus. It is located between the upper part of the vagina and the uterus.

3. Ovaries: These can be found on the sides of the uterus and are about the size of a walnut. Ovaries release female hormones that help a girl's body develop. They also release an egg cell each month, at which time a girl will get her period.

4. Fallopian Tubes: These two tubes are attached to the upper part of each side of the uterus. Each one is about four inches long. The egg passes from the Fallopian tubes into the uterus.

5. Vagina: This is the forward opening between your legs. It is also called the birth canal. When a baby is born, it passes through the stretched vagina. This is also where tampons are inserted when a woman begins menstruating.

6. Hymen: This is a piece of tissue that surrounds the opening of the vagina. Since the hymen is very flexible, using tampons will not hurt it.

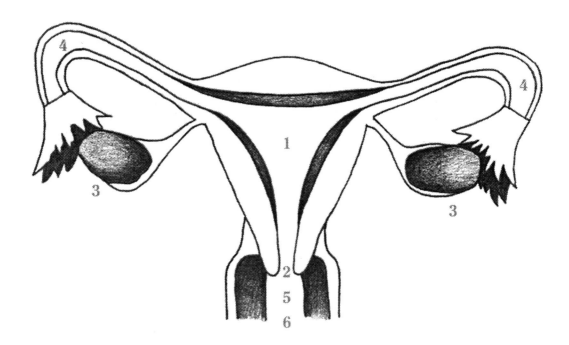

Menstruation

This is the time in your life when you will start having your period—menstruating. No one can tell you exactly when this will begin, except that it usually starts two years after you notice your breasts developing. Ask your mother at what age she got her first period. Chances are this is when you'll get yours.

Being ready for your period will help you feel more comfortable about it. If your parents haven't told you about beginning your menstrual cycle, you may want to ask them questions about it or ask them to buy you a book that will help you understand it better.

What happens when I menstruate?

A very small egg leaves one of your ovaries (1, 2). This egg floats down through the Fallopian tube (3, 4).

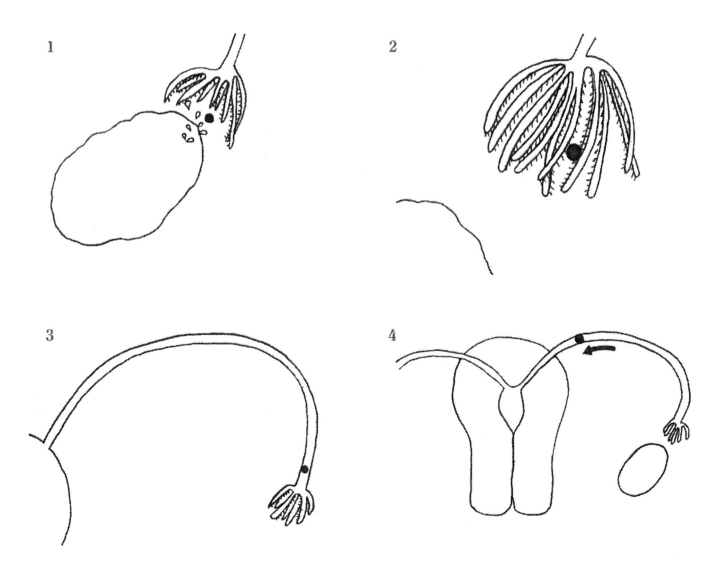

While this is happening, your uterus is building up a lining of fresh tissue and blood. If a man's sperm enters the egg, fertilization occurs and the woman becomes pregnant. If the egg is not fertilized, the lining in your uterus, which is made up of blood and tissue, comes out through your vagina (6, 7). This is called having your period.

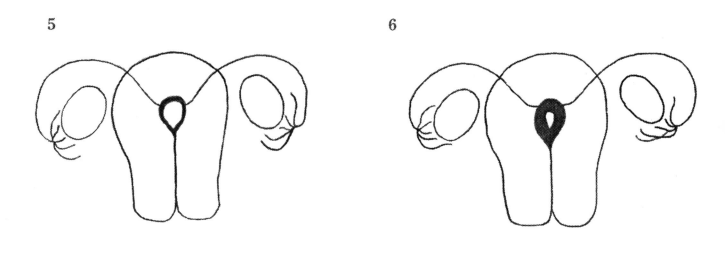

Two weeks after this, your body is again getting ready for another egg to pass through, and the same things happen all over again (8). This is called your menstrual cycle, and the entire process takes about a month. This cycle will continue in your life until you are about forty or fifty years old.

Your period may last as few as two or as many as eight days. Each girl is different.

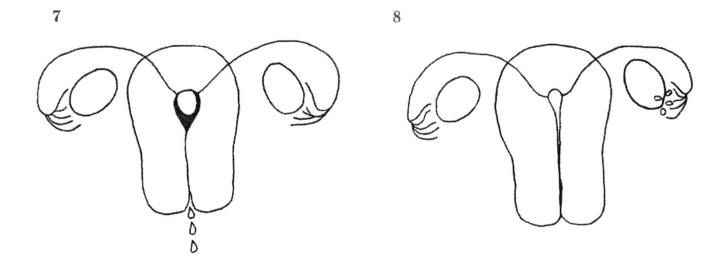

What do I use for my period?

Many girls and women use sanitary pads (also called sanitary napkins) which can be purchased in any drugstore, supermarket, or health and beauty store. These pads come in various sizes and thicknesses. Ask your mother to help you select one that suits your needs. Like many girls, you may feel funny wearing a pad at first. But you'll get used to it. Keep in mind that no one can tell you're wearing one.

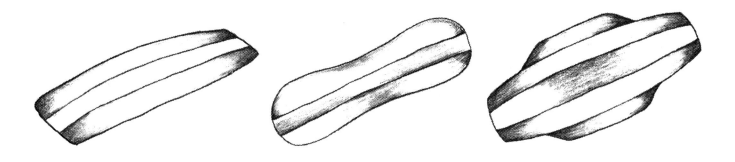

Tampons are another method used by many girls and women to catch their menstrual flow. One kind of tampon looks like a small tube and is made of soft cotton which is pressed together with a string attached to one end.

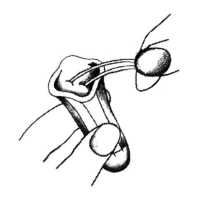 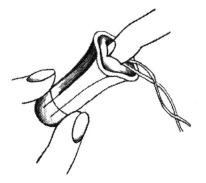

Preparing the tampon for use: pull strings to one side, insert finger into end.

Another kind is also made of soft cotton but is inserted with the tube.

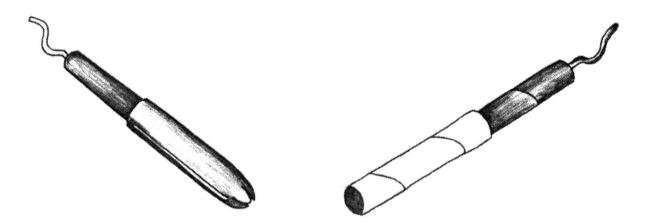

The tampon fits inside the vagina with the string hanging down outside of the vagina. To remove the tampon, pull gently on the string and it will slowly slide out. Do not leave a tampon in for more than a few hours, as this can lead to toxic shock syndrome, a serious condition. It's very important that you read the directions that come with the tampons to ensure that you use them properly.

Change your tampon regularly throughout the day, and don't leave a tampon in at night while sleeping. Use a sanitary pad instead.

To prevent odor, keep small zip-lock plastic bags in your bathroom and purse so you can wrap your sanitary pads and tampons before putting them in a wastebasket.

What are some of the side effects of menstrual cycles?

Some girls don't have side effects, but others do. Some of these may include headaches, backaches, mood changes, depression, cramps, water retention, bloating, nausea, and a tired feeling.

These symptoms are referred to by some people as PMS, which means premenstrual syndrome. There are several things you can do to help yourself feel better if you experience these symptoms:

- ♥ Right before your period begins, lower your salt intake. This will discourage your body from retaining excess water, which can cause swelling, tension, and depression.
- ♥ Maintain a balanced diet.
- ♥ Get plenty of sleep.
- ♥ Exercise. Many people believe this helps prevent or relieve painful cramps.
- ♥ Avoid sweetened drinks, chocolate, junk food, and sugar.
- ♥ If your periods are painful, ask your mother to talk with your doctor. The doctor may recommend special vitamin and mineral supplements.
- ♥ To keep from tensing up when you have a cramp, breathe deeply and slowly.
- ♥ Take a warm bath to help you relax.

Remember, there's nothing wrong with you when you feel different right before your period. Many girls find that talking about it with friends helps, because they find their friends have some of the same symptoms. And keep in mind that these symptoms usually become less frequent as you get older.

Notes

EXERCISE

In 1992 Arnold Schwarzenegger was a special guest at a school where I was teaching fourth grade. Arnold had asked to exercise with a fourth grade class, and I was surprised and pleased when my class was chosen for the honor.

Arnold was not only Chairman of the President's Council on Physical Fitness and Sports, but he was also very devoted to helping kids learn proper nutrition and exercise. I was fascinated with his drive and determination to be the best he could be, and with his desire to help kids do the same.

During the session, Arnold stressed the importance of proper eating habits as well as a good exercise program. He feels school physical education classes and organized sports programs cannot replace your own personal exercise program. "They do not provide enough exercise," Arnold said. He believes kids should do some kind of aerobic activity for twenty-five minutes, every other day. Needless to say, I agree with Arnold 100 percent.

I felt very honored meeting Arnold Schwarzenegger.

A Home Exercise Routine Just For You

Warm-up (5 minutes)

(Warming up helps prevent stiffness and injuries.)

1. Stretching from toe to toe and side to side.
2. Jumping jacks.

Head Rolls

Rotate your head to the right and around, twice. Do the same going to the left.

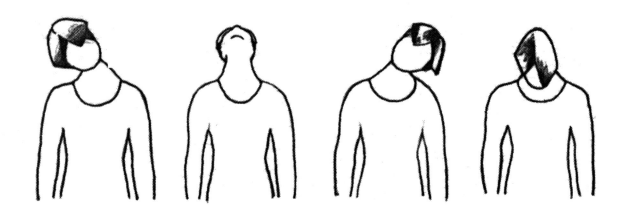

Chest and Shoulder Stretch

Clasp your hands together behind you. Raise your arms up as far as you can. Hold and count to 5 without arching your back.

Side Bends

With your right arm, reach up and stretch to the left as far as you can. Count to 5. Do the opposite with your left arm. Do this eight times on each side.

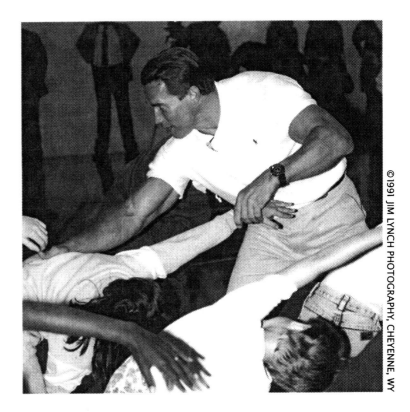

Arnold is very devoted to helping children learn about proper exercise.

Twist That Waist

With your feet apart and knees bent slightly, twist your arms from right to left. Do not move your hips. Do this 8 times.

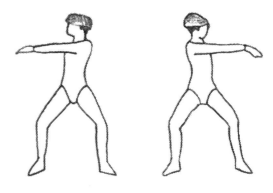

Stretching the Hamstrings

I. Lean over forward, bending your knees slightly. Bend over and down until hands are on your legs. Count to 8. Do this 4 times. (Your feet should be shoulder-width apart.)

II. Bend down over your right leg. Count to 8. Bend down over your left leg; count to 8. Do this 4 times on each side. (Again, your feet should be shoulder-width apart.)

Stomach Curls

While lying on your back, press your lower back into the floor. Lift your knees to your chest, while keeping your hands behind your head. Do this 8 times.

Toning Your Stomach

While lying on your back, place your hands under your buttocks. Lift your legs to the same level as your hips, then spread your legs out to the sides. Bring them back and cross them like a scissors. Do this 10 times, switching legs each time you cross them.

Leg Lifts

Lie on one side with your legs slightly bent. Push your hips somewhat forward, keeping your body straight. Lift your top leg up and down 10 times, then switch to other side and do 10 more.

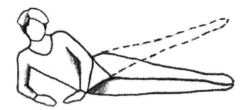

Thigh Toning

Get down on your hands and knees and put your right leg out to the side and lift it as high as you can. Keep your knee straight and your foot flexed, so you stretch your hamstring muscle on the back of your thigh. Raise and lower your leg 10 times. Now make 10 circles forward and 10 backward with your leg. Do the same thing with the left leg the same number of times. (Also known as "The Doggy"!)

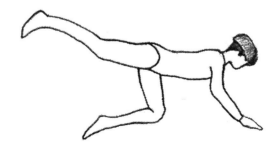

Toning Your Buttocks

I. Sit on the floor with your legs straight but relaxed. Your back should also be straight. "Walk" forward on your buttocks using their muscles, tightening them as you move forward. After sliding several steps forward, slide back again, tightening as you slide. Do this 5 or 6 times.

II. (1) Lie on the floor with your knees bent and your legs slightly apart. Press your lower back into the floor as you lift and squeeze the buttock muscle. Repeat 8 times.

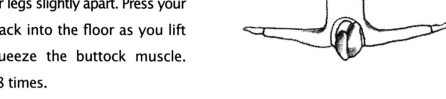

(2) Bring your knees together and then pull them out. Squeeze your buttocks upwards as your knees come together, and release it as your knees open. Repeat 8 times.

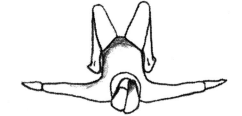

(3) Bounce your knees with a back and forth motion for 16 counts. Squeeze your buttock muscle upward during the entire 16 counts. Your lower back should be pressed into the floor.

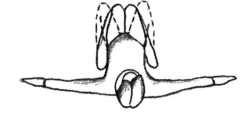

Relaxing the Spine

Lie on the floor with your arms out at your sides. Bring your knees to your chest. Slowly lower your knees to one side while your head turns to the other side. Exhale while you do this. Count to 10. Repeat on the other side. Do both sides 20 times.

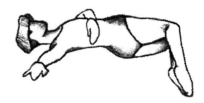

Cool Down

Do a few slow stretches, swinging your arms back and forth, for 2–3 minutes. Don't you feel better? I'm sure you do.

This entire routine should not take longer than 20–30 minutes. Play your favorite cassette or CD while you exercise to help make it fun.

Helpful Hints

- ♥ Keep a consistent exercise schedule rather than starting and then stopping. Staying on a regular schedule will give you much better results.
- ♥ If you are overweight, check with your doctor before starting an exercise program.
- ♥ Don't exercise if you have an injury. Let it heal and then start again.
- ♥ Other ways of exercising are jogging, walking, biking, rollerblading, swimming, and playing tennis or racquetball.
- ♥ Exercising with friends will make your workout more enjoyable.
- ♥ Always try to breathe properly when exercising. Exhale when you are stretching. Inhale when you are relaxing.
- ♥ Concentrate on each exercise. Try to do it as perfectly as you can.
- ♥ Start exercising for a short time when starting. Increase your time as you become stronger.

Notes

HEALTH & FITNESS

Cleaning Your Body

As you grow older, you sweat more and therefore develop body odor. You will sweat under your arms, between your legs around your genital area, and other places.

It's important that you wash regularly. Make sure you clean your genital area. Standing under the shower or soaking in a tub of water isn't going to completely clean you. Use a washcloth. Put soap on it and wash your body. Then rinse. Apply body lotion while you are partly wet. This will help keep moisture in your skin.

Wearing Deodorant

Since you are at the age when sweating occurs, it's necessary for you to use a deodorant. It will help control odor and help cut down on your sweating.

When my daughter started using a deodorant she had a hard time finding a suitable one for her, because she broke out in a rash from using many brands. Finally, we visited a dermatologist to find out what she was allergic to before buying the next brand, and eventually she found one she could use without causing her skin to become irritated.

If you have a skin reaction to your new deodorant, don't hesitate to ask your parents to take you to a dermatologist. He can help you choose one that's right for you.

Another helpful bit of advice is knowing how to put it on. A dermatologist once told me that the gland in the center of your armpit is the size of a quarter. That area is the only spot where deodorant should be applied. Many people put deodorant in their whole armpit area plus part of their arm. This can cause skin dryness and itching.

Wearing Clean Clothes

Always wear clean clothes. You will not smell clean after you shower if you put on dirty clothes. This is especially true with underwear. Wearing dirty under-clothes will still cause you to smell, no matter how clean you are.

Your clothes don't have to be expensive or new, just clean.

Cleaning Your Face

You are born with beautiful skin. What it looks like as you get older is determined by how well you take care of it now. A good skin care program, especially cleansing, toning and moisturizing, is extremely important.

Skin Types

The type of skin you have determines the way you should take care of your complexion. The following guidelines should help if you have problems deciding which type you have.

Oily: Your complexion seems shiny. Large pores are easily seen all over your face and you will get blackheads and whiteheads frequently.

Dry: Your complexion will have a dull look to it. Blackheads and whiteheads will not appear often. At times your skin will itch.

T-Zone: If your skin is dry in all areas except your forehead, nose, and chin, you have combination-type skin. Pores will show only in the T-zone and you will usually get blackheads and white-heads only in that area.

If you can't decide which skin type you have, try this: First thing in the morning, tear a tissue into four pieces. Press a piece against your forehead for twelve seconds. If it shows any type of soil or if it sticks to your head, your skin is oily. If it shows no change, your skin is dry. Do the same on your cheeks, chin, and nose to see if you have combination skin.

What If I Have Oily Skin?

1. Not taking care of excess oil can cause skin problems. You should wash your face gently two or three times daily. An oil-free soap or non-oily facial cleanser is best.
2. Use an alcohol-based astringent every day on oily areas only.
3. Be careful not to get hair spray on your face. This, plus bangs, may lead to oil buildup, which causes blemishes.

What If I Have Dry Skin?

1. Use a gentle soap or cleanser that moisturizes—it will help remove dirt.
2. A rich moisturizer should be used during the day and at night.
3. Having a humidifier in your bedroom will also help keep your skin moist, especially if you live in a dry climate.

What If I Have T-Zone Combination Skin?

Use the same steps for oily skin on your forehead, nose, and chin. Use the treatment for dry skin on the remainder of your face. Using astringent on your forehead, nose, and chin will help absorb excess oil. Using moisturizer on the drier cheek areas will help soften the skin.

Recommended Skin Care Program (Do Twice Daily):

1. Pin hair away from face.
2. Use a facial soap or cream for your type of skin. Gently wash forehead, cheeks, chin, jawline, and neck. Do not rub or tug skin. Rinse with cool (not cold) water and pat dry.
3. Put a small amount of astringent on a cotton ball and use on oily areas only.
4. Apply a small amount of lotion to dry areas.
5. Never go to bed without washing your face!

CHAPTER 9

What Products Do I Buy?

I, along with many dermatologists, discourage teens from spending money on high cost items when there are many inexpensive yet excellent products available at most drug stores and health and beauty stores.

Check with your school nurse or family doctor about what she may recommend. The following are good choices.

Cetaphil: A great face wash.

Witch Hazel: An astringent to help absorb any leftover makeup or excess oil.

Almay: A hypoallergenic brand name lotion to use on dry areas of the skin.

Pimples

One of the signs of puberty is pimples or acne. That's because oil glands enlarge and an oily substance, called sebum, is present beneath the skin. Extra sebum causes whiteheads or blackheads. This infection causes pimples. If the infection is severe, you may have to consult a dermatologist, because medication will help the healing process.

I remember when a former student of mine visited me. He had a terrible case of acne on his face—his pimples were red and infected and there were many of them. When he talked with me he kept looking down at the floor. I could tell he was very self-conscious of the way he looked. When I spoke to his mother later, she said she wasn't aware that a dermatologist could prescribe medication to help her son. I assured her that it would help. They put him on a special program, gave him medicine, and my former

student's face cleared up remarkably well. The only problem was some scarring from other acne, because he waited too long before consulting a doctor.

So don't let your acne get out of control. See a doctor if your skin becomes badly infected or if your acne doesn't go away. You can control the acne, but not the scars. You live with those forever. That's why it is important not to wait too long before consulting a doctor.

Skin Care Tips

- ♥ Do not pick or squeeze blackheads or pimples.
- ♥ Do not touch your face with dirty hands.
- ♥ Don't put your hands on your face while using the telephone.
- ♥ Rinse thoroughly after washing.
- ♥ Drink 6–8 glasses of water daily.
- ♥ Get plenty of exercise.
- ♥ Maintain a well-balanced diet.
- ♥ Maintain good toilet habits by washing your hands after using the bathroom.
- ♥ Get 8 hours of sleep each night.
- ♥ Maintain a happy attitude.
- ♥ Wash off any makeup before going to bed.

Let The Sun Be Your Good Friend

The sun's rays can damage your skin if you don't know the right sunscreen to use or how to apply it. Here are some helpful hints:

1. Use sunscreen with an SPF (Sun Protection Factor) high enough for your skin type. SPF 15 or higher is made for people who have fair skin and who burn often and easily.

2. If you tan easily without burning, try SPF 10.

3. If your skin is sensitive, or if you have had a bad reaction from sunscreens in the past, choose a sunscreen that has no fragrance and no para-aminobenzoic acid (PABA) in it.

4. Choose an oil-free sunscreen if you get pimples easily.

5. Apply sunscreen half an hour before dressing to go out in the sun.

6. Reapply sunscreen every two hours.

7. Use a sunscreen specifically designed for your face and eyes. If you don't you may feel some stinging and burning if sunscreen gets in your eyes.

8. Being in the shade doesn't protect you from the sun. You can still get burned from the sun's reflection, and the sun's rays penetrating through your clothing. Try to wear a sunscreen whenever you are going to be outside for a long time.

9. Make sure you put sunscreen on sensitive areas like your nose, cheekbones, ears, and shoulders.

Getting A Suntanned Appearance Without The Sun

You may think a little tan looks and feels great, but more sun does not make for more beautiful skin. In fact, it makes your skin more susceptible to wrinkling as you age—and, worst of all, it can cause skin cancer. Damage from sunburn occurring before age 12 may affect skin cancer development in later years.

If you don't want to damage your skin, but you want the pretty glow that a tan gives, create your own. There are several products on the market that can help you get a suntanned look.

These products, when applied periodically, will give you the appearance of a tan, and they're approved by dermatologists as being safe. Check with a cosmetic department to find out which is best for your skin type.

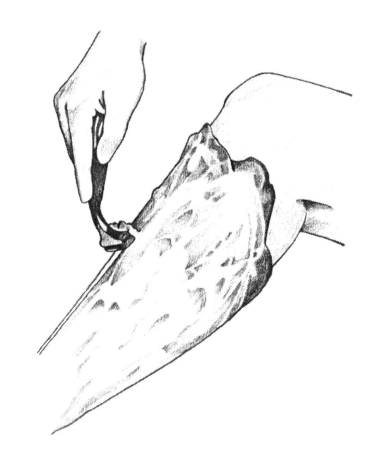

Body Hair

You'll notice hair growing on various parts of your body when going through puberty—underarms and legs and the upper lip and chin. Some hair in these areas is normal. The amount of body hair you have is inherited—your mother or grandmother may have had hair appear in the same places as you do.

Whether to remove certain areas of hair on your body is up to you and your parents. Shaving your underarms will certainly make you feel less vulnerable to body odor. Shaving your legs is something you may or may not want to do. If the hair is very light in color and there isn't much of it, you may choose not to remove it. On the other hand, if it's dark and thick and you don't like the looks of it, you may discuss this with your mother and let her know how you feel.

Shaving

This is done on underarms, legs, and bikini lines. Do NOT shave any area on your face. Shaving can be done once or twice a week, depending on how fast your hair grows.

Use a fresh, sharp razor that hasn't been used by anyone else. Do not try to shave your legs when they're dry. Wet them and apply a shaving cream over your entire lower leg, up to just past the knee cap.

Place the razor in the direction opposite the growth of your hair and pull it up toward you in long, even strokes. Rinse off the razor after every 2–3 strokes.

Apply your favorite body lotion when you're finished.

Eyebrows

When tweezing extra hair from your brow, try not to change the natural shape of the brow itself. Many girls don't know how to tweeze properly, so they remove brows that shouldn't be removed. After several years these brows don't grow back, making it difficult to shape the remaining ones.

Ask the person who cuts your hair at your styling salon to help you decide which hairs to remove.

The beginning of the eyebrow should be in line with the inner corner of the eye and end just beyond the eye. You may want to remove a few hairs from one brow, and then do the other one. This eliminates over-tweezing and allows you to see if the brows are balanced.

You want a soft arch (not a peak) at the top of your brow.

Directions For Tweezing:

1. Clean the eye area and lubricate the skin to soften the area.
2. Using an eyebrow brush, brush brows into their natural shape.
3. Use one hand to pull skin snugly back.
4. Tweeze one hair at a time, going in the brow direction. You want to remove any hairs that lie outside your natural brow shape.
5. Brush the eyebrow in place with a brow brush.

Clean Teeth

I remember a visit to the dentist when I was younger. He said to brush twice daily, and never forget to floss each night. I thought I would never be able to find the time. Now I laugh about it and think how silly I was.

Once you get used to it, you'd be surprised how little time it takes to take care of your teeth. Brushing your teeth removes plaque buildup. Flossing helps get out food in between your teeth and around your gums. Many people today have good teeth, but lose them because their gums are so worn down from plaque buildup that their teeth fall out. You can floss while studying or even watching TV. Just don't do it in front of others.

Have someone help you schedule an appointment to visit your dentist at least twice a year. He or she will clean and check your teeth and answer any questions you may have about how to care for them. This is especially important if you wear braces.

Caring For Your Hands

Your hands tell people a lot about yourself. If you care for your body, you will take the time to file and clean your nails.

1. Always remove old nail polish.

2. To avoid damage and splitting nails, it's very important that you learn to file properly. Using an emery board, file your nails in one direction. File from one side of your nail toward the center. Don't file the corners of your nail; this will only weaken it. File the tops of your nails in one direction also. Use the smooth side of your file for more fragile nails.

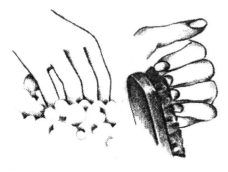

3. Soak your nails for two minutes in warm soapy water. Dirt and stains can be removed gently with a nail brush.

4. You may use a hand lotion at this time to soften cuticles (skin from the back of each nail). You can push your cuticles back while they are wet by using a wet washcloth. Put a finger underneath the washcloth and push gently. A nail clipper can be used at this time to remove any hangnails.

If your nails have a tendency to peel, a light coat of clear polish can help prevent this.

Nail Biting

I have several students each year who are nail biters. They do it because they're bored, nervous, or just because it's a habit. There are several things you can do to help prevent nail biting.

1. Find something to do with your hands if you are relaxing or watching TV.

2. Use a product sold in drug stores that looks like nail polish but it tastes awful. The directions will tell you how to use it.

3. Give yourself a manicure (mentioned in this chapter). Girls have told me that when they take care of their nails, they don't feel like biting them any longer.

4. Don't feel frustrated if you can't break the habit overnight, especially if you've been doing it for awhile. Work on it a day at a time.

Caring For Your Feet

Your feet probably take the most abuse of any part of your body.

Soaking your feet in warm water for 15 minutes can help you feel great all over. It will also help soften corns or calluses. After soaking, these can be removed with a pumice stone by rubbing in a circular motion. Apply body lotion afterward to keep soles and toes soft.

When clipping your toenails, remember to clip them straight across.

Adolescents and adults experience problems with their feet. Most of these problems can be avoided if you follow these few basic precautions:

1. Never wear shoes that don't fit properly. Corns, calluses, bone distortions, and other problems may result.

2. Always wear rubber thongs or some form of foot protection when using a public shower.

3. Put foot powder in your shoes if you have a problem with foot odor or itching.

4. Do not wear pantyhose that are too short.

5. Give yourself a foot massage now and then. Rub your favorite lotion into your feet and then sit with your feet propped up.

Clean Hair

I mentioned earlier that your hair needs to be cleaned more often because of oil buildup. Shampoo your hair regularly. If you don't, it will look stringy and also smell bad.

The hairstyle you choose should be one that suits you. Don't wear your hair a certain way just because most kids in your class wear it that way. Develop your own style, one that makes you attractive, feels comfortable, and fits your personality. Ask a stylist to help you choose one if you're undecided about the style that's best for your face.

What To Do With What You Have

Knowing the condition and texture of your hair is extremely helpful when purchasing hair care products. I recall that friends in college would complain because they had great hair but couldn't seem to style it without a lot of trouble. Most of them were using the wrong shampoo and entirely too much conditioner. This made their hair heavy, greasy, and very unmanageable.

Be sure to read the information on hair product bottles or cans before purchasing them. If you can't decide, ask a stylist about what's best for your hair type.

Shampoo And Condition

Shampoo your hair whenever necessary. Wet your hair, put a small amount of shampoo in the palm of your hand, and distribute it evenly over your entire scalp area. Massage your scalp with your fingertips. Shampoo long hair by leaning over and lathering it with your hands. Rinse well. Shampoo left in your hair will make it look dull.

Conditioner can be applied after excess water is squeezed from your hair. Wrap your hair loosely in a towel. Pat the towel on your hair to help dry it. To avoid damaging your hair, do not pull or tug on it while it is wet. Use a comb, never a brush, to comb out wet hair.

Conditioners are used as follows:

1.   *Instant Conditioners*—Used immediately after shampooing to help make hair smooth and shiny.

2.   *Deep Conditioners*—These are left on for 15–30 minutes. They penetrate the hair shaft, helping to repair damaged parts of the hair.

Read the directions on shampoo and conditioners

to help you decide what will work best for your type of hair. This will save money on unused products and prevent you from buying the wrong product for your hair.

To Perm Or Not To Perm

Before you decide to perm your hair, you should consult a stylist, because your hair type and its condition are critical. A perm is more successful on long, thick, coarse hair than on fine, short hair. Using smaller rollers will determine how curly your hair will get. The type of solution used will determine the tightness of the curl. After deciding what type of perm is best for you, find out what kind of shampoo and conditioner you should use and how you should take care of permed hair.

Helpful Hint: If you want to see what a permed look is like on you, roll your wet hair on perm rollers and allow it to dry. This way you'll know for sure if you like that look.

What Is The Condition Of Your Hair?

1. *Dry Hair:* Breaks easily, has many split ends, very fly-away.
2. *Oily Hair:* Separates easily, feels limp and heavy, sticks together, doesn't curl well.
3. *Normal Hair:* Smooth, has a nice shine. Doesn't appear dry or oily.

What Is The Texture Of Your Hair?

1. *Coarse:* Thick and wiry looking.
2. *Medium:* Neither coarse, wiry, fly-away, or fine.
1. *Fine:* Baby-like in texture. Hard to curl. Very fly-away.

The Haircut

Stylists recommend you trim your hair every six to eight weeks to maintain a healthy, shapely look. Let a stylist know how your hair behaves, and tell her of any problems you may have styling it. Many girls take a picture that they've clipped from a magazine to give their stylists some idea of how they want their hair cut. I recommend taking two or three pictures along, in case one style does not work for your facial shape or hair type.

Don't schedule your hair appointment before a special event. You may not be happy with the way it turns out, and wearing that style to a special occasion could be embarrassing for you.

Remember, a haircut always looks better after a few days. You should also give yourself a week or two to get used to a style if it is really different from the last cut and style you had. If you are totally unhappy, make an appointment with your stylist for suggestions on a change.

A Word Of Caution About Chlorine

Swimming is wonderful exercise, but it can also damage your hair. Chlorine not only bleaches hair, but can change its natural color and cause split ends. Wet your hair, then wear a swim cap—and wash your hair immediately after swimming, before it dries. Ask your stylist to recommend a product which can be sprayed on your hair before swimming to prevent damage.

Dandruff

Excess shampoo left in your hair, an incorrect diet, or certain medications can all cause dandruff. If you notice an itchy feeling on your scalp and flaking on your shoulders, you may want to investigate some of the products designed specifically to get rid of dandruff.

If this doesn't work, or the flaking increases, ask your parents to take you to a doctor who can prescribe a special shampoo to clear up the dandruff.

Remember:

1. Keep brushes clean by washing them in warm soapy water at least once a week.
2. 100 strokes a day is out! Brush your hair only as much as you need to.
3. If you have fly-away hair, put a small amount of hair spray on your brush.
4. Never brush your hair when it's wet—use a wide-toothed comb.
5. If you're not sure which brush to use, consult your stylist.
6. Instead of always using a blow dryer, let your hair dry naturally as much as possible.
7. If your hair is breaking or especially dry, use a deep conditioner.
8. Whenever possible, cover your hair with a scarf or hat when in the sun.
9. Do not use plain rubber bands or barrettes with sharp edges. Both can damage your hair. Use the fabric-coated kind—many attractive designs are available.
10. If you're not comfortable with your hairstyle, don't be afraid to have a stylist help you choose another.

Products And Gadgets For Styling Your Hair

Electric Rollers	Use for a loose soft set. Place quite a few strands of hair on each roller. Test a roller every few minutes to make sure hair isn't too curly.
Curling Iron	Wind hair around the wand. Keep it away from your face so you don't burn yourself. Unwind your hair when you feel you have a tight enough curl.
Crimping Iron	Use for spot-crimping hair.
Blow Drying	A quick and easy way to dry hair. When used without electric rollers or a curling iron, blow drying will definitely straighten hair. Some girls use a diffuser attachment on their blow dryers to smooth hair that's too curly.

NOTE: Do not hold the blow dryer too close to your hair. Also, don't turn on the hottest setting or your hair will eventually become dry and susceptible to split ends. |
Sponge Rollers	Creates extra volume; must be left in until hair is dry.
Pin Curls	Adds volume. Large pin curls will create waves. Put in when hair is wet, and let dry.
Hair Spray	Keeps your hairstyle in place and helps control fly-away hair. For fullness, bend over at the waist and spray under your hair. Wait 5–7 seconds. Stand up and style your hair lightly. Finish by spraying a small amount of hair spray on your hair. Too much hair spray will dry your hair; use it sparingly.
Mousse	Gives body to your hair and lets you style and shape it without leaving it stiff or sticky. Apply to towel-dried hair. Place mousse on your hair roots. Blow dry. If you blow dry from the roots by pushing hair away from your face, you will get more height to your style. Your stylist can teach you how to use mousse.

Exercise

Whether you play sports, lift weights, swim or ski, exercise should become part of your weekly routine. Try different activities and change your exercise. Making them enjoyable will help keep your

Notes

Nutrition

How healthy you are and will be later on in life depends on what you eat in your early years. Good nutrition and plenty of exercise are important health habits you should begin today. Just like learning to read and write helps you become educated, learning how to eat properly will help you develop a healthy body into your adult years.

Do you remember a time when you didn't have much food in your stomach? Or a time when you ate only sweets for two days? You probably felt miserable, crabby, and even depressed. Well, that's why good nutrition is so important. If you're not feeling well or you're not eating right you may also be unhappy and feel weak. In time, this state can lead to clinical depression.

We've all heard the saying that "you are what you eat." Eating a lot of sweets and other unhealthy foods will certainly cause you to feel a loss of energy and act cranky. I mentioned in the self-esteem chapter that feeling good is liking yourself and taking care of who you are. Eating properly is one way to accomplish that.

You probably remember hearing about the food groups in school. For example, the foods in the milk group supply calcium, vitamins, and proteins to help build teeth and bones. You should eat about three servings daily.

Eggs, peanut butter, cheese, fish, and lean meats give you protein, iron and vitamins to help you grow and to build your muscles. They also help your blood.

Vegetables and fruits have special vitamins and minerals to help your skin and eyes.

Breads, cereals, and pasta provide carbohydrates, fiber, vitamins, and iron that give you energy and keep you from being tired.

Several years ago the United States Department of Agriculture issued new nutritional guidelines which they refer to as the Food Pyramid. Their emphasis is on complex carbohydrates and less emphasis on animal fat.

If you're not sure which foods you need or how much you need from each group, look at the following chart for guidelines.

The Basic Food Groups

To help you decide what foods are best for you, read the following information on the Five Basic Food Groups. It will help you decide what you should eat each day to maintain a healthy diet.

1. Meat, Poultry, Fish, Dry Beans, Eggs, and Nuts

Fish, eggs, cheese, peanut butter and tofu are a few choices—2–3 servings a day.

2. Fruits

This includes all fruit—2–4 servings a day.

3. Vegetables

This includes green and other low-calorie vegetables. Green beans, broccoli, cauliflower, and celery are a few—3–5 servings a day.

4. Bread, Cereal, Rice, and Pasta

This food group includes cooked cereal as well—6–11 servings a day.

5. Milk, Yogurt, and Cheese

You may have natural cheese or processed cheese—2–3 servings a day.

*   Fats, Oils; and Sweets

This is not a food group. It would be wise to limit your servings.

At times we are responsible for fixing our own meals or planning our own meal times. This is good practice, and helps you become aware of good eating habits.

Below is a guide to go by. A chart is also provided for you so you can plan your eating time following the five food groups plan.

With the help of your mother or the person who prepares the meals in your house, write down an eating plan—and stick to it. Tack your personal eating guide to the bulletin board in your room, or tape it to a mirror. You may even want to post it on the refrigerator door, if no one objects.

The following is an example of what your plan might look like, along with a blank chart which you can photocopy and fill in with your own personal eating plan.

MONDAY	TUESDAY	WEDNESDAY	THURSDAY	FRIDAY
Breakfast	**Breakfast**	**Breakfast**	**Breakfast**	**Breakfast**
Juice Cereal & milk w/sliced strawberries	Milk 2 scrambled eggs Low-fat sausage 2 slices of toast	Milk 2 toasted waffles Low-fat sausage Banana	Juice 2-egg cheese omelet 1 slice cheese 1 slice toast	Juice 2 English muffins with peanut butter Grapes
Lunch	**Lunch**	**Lunch**	**Lunch**	**Lunch**
Milk Vegetarian pizza Banana	Milk Chicken sandwich with lettuce Apple	Fruit juice 2 pieces chicken Steamed vegetables Apple	Milk Macaroni and cheese Veg. salad Cantaloupe	Milk Cheeseburger Potato chips Orange
Dinner	**Dinner**	**Dinner**	**Dinner**	**Dinner**
Milk Chicken Banana Vegetable	Milk Meat loaf Pear Vegetable	Milk Fish Peach Vegetable	Milk Chicken Strawberries Vegetable	Milk Roast beef Apple Vegetable

Helpful Hints

- ♥ You may want to add:
  1. Rice
  2. Baked potato
  3. Hot noodles
  4. Fresh or frozen veggies

- ♥ A quick salad that goes with either poultry or fish:

Put 2 halved, canned (or fresh) peaches on a bed of lettuce. Fill each half with cranberry orange relish.

- ♥ A tasty salad that goes well with ham or fish:

Put 2 halves of canned (or fresh) pears on a bed of lettuce. Fill each half with

cottage cheese. Top with a maraschino cherry.

- ♥ Other good salad choices:

Slices of apples, celery sticks, and carrot sticks or canned fruit cocktail.

♥ Instead of eating rich desserts after meals, try eating different fruits and cheeses.

♥ Have a file of your favorite, easy recipes so you can fix your own meal if you have to, or so you can treat your mom and dad sometime when they're tired.

♥ For a special event, use matching place mats and cloth napkins. Use your mom's favorite small houseplant as a centerpiece.

♥ Play your mom or dad's favorite tape or CD as background music for a special dinner event. Try to think of interesting things to discuss while eating.

A Word Of Caution About Fast Foods

Fast foods have a lot of fat and salt in them. Buy a small calorie pocket book— look through it and memorize the calories in two or three of your favorite fast foods. You may also want to check the chart below and jot down the number of calories in the things you eat most often.

When you go to a fast food restaurant, choose the burger, fries, or nuggets that have the fewest calories and least salt to cut your calorie and salt intake. Excess salt intake can cause premenstrual water retention, high blood pressure, and strokes.

FAST FOOD CALORIES		
French fries:	large	360
	regular	210
Burger:	regular	265
	large (Whopper, Big Mac)	600
Chicken:	6 nuggets	320
	1 piece fried chicken	200
Taco		190
Chocolate shake		450
Pizza slice		180–200
(with cheese, tomato, pepper, mushroom)		

Snacking To Stay Healthy

For years snacking was considered unhealthy, and parents tried to stop their kids from eating between meals. But this thinking has changed, and today both adults and kids are learning that snacking can actually be good for them.

Nutritious snacks can supply your body with many healthy foods you may not be getting enough of at your regular mealtimes. Also, eating regular snacks can help control your appetite so you won't overeat at mealtimes.

The two key points to remember when snacking are:

1. Nutrition—Choose a snack that's wholesome and nutritious, not one that's high in calories, fat, or sugar. Foods like candy bars, hot fudge sundaes, or potato chips provide "empty calories" and have very little or no nutritional value.

2. Moderation—There is no connection between your body weight and the number of times you eat during the day. You gain weight only when you eat more calories than your body uses for energy (3,500 calories = 1 pound). So to control your weight, don't worry so much about when you eat but always watch what you eat and how much you eat, although it's better to eat the majority of your food before 8 p.m.

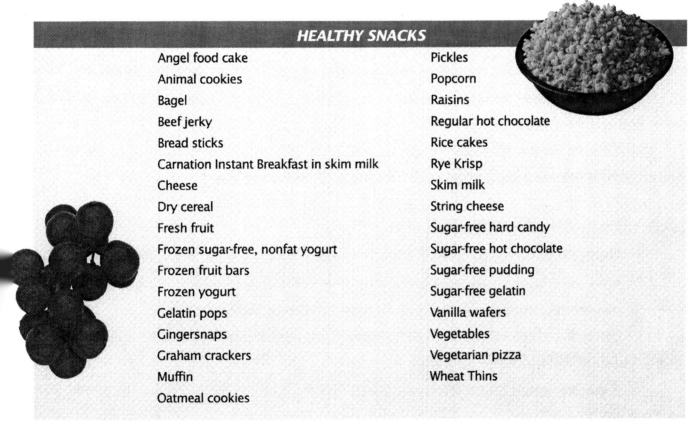

HEALTHY SNACKS

Angel food cake	Pickles
Animal cookies	Popcorn
Bagel	Raisins
Beef jerky	Regular hot chocolate
Bread sticks	Rice cakes
Carnation Instant Breakfast in skim milk	Rye Krisp
Cheese	Skim milk
Dry cereal	String cheese
Fresh fruit	Sugar-free hard candy
Frozen sugar-free, nonfat yogurt	Sugar-free hot chocolate
Frozen fruit bars	Sugar-free pudding
Frozen yogurt	Sugar-free gelatin
Gelatin pops	Vanilla wafers
Gingersnaps	Vegetables
Graham crackers	Vegetarian pizza
Muffin	Wheat Thins
Oatmeal cookies	

A Word Of Caution About Fad Diets

Yes, you can lose weight on a fad diet. Most of the time, however, this weight will not stay off. You lose the weight and then in a few days it's back. This is why it happens:

When people go on fad diets (usually 1,000 calories or less) they are choosing to fast, so they don't take in the necessary amount of fuel their bodies need. A fasting body will do the following things to meet its energy needs:

1. As the fast begins, glucose from the liver's stored glycogen and the fatty acids from the body's stored fat both flow into the body's cells for fuel.

2. After several hours, most of the liver's glycogen stores are used up.

3. At this time, most cells depend on the body's stored fat to provide fuel.

4. The brain cells need a minimum of 400–600 calories daily, but they can't use the body's stored fats—they still need glucose. This presents a problem for the person who is fasting.

5. In order to get the necessary fuel to the brain and nervous system, the fasting body breaks down its vital protein tissue in the muscles and changes it to glucose.

6. As the muscles waste away, they do less work, so the loss of body fat at this point is very little.

7. After this, the weight lost in fad dieting is not fat. It is mostly glycogen and protein, as well as water and important minerals.

8. Once off the diet, the body will quickly hold on to the needed materials it lost during the fast, and the weight will come back, often to the starting point before the diet.

Healthy Hints For Good Eating

♥ More calories are added to food when it's topped with oily sauces or sugared toppings.

♥ If you need to limit calories, eat what you usually do but cut your food intake in half.

♥ To curb your appetite, drink a glass of water 10 minutes before your meal.

♥ You may want to keep carrot sticks or celery in a small plastic bag and put it in your school locker. Munch on these during break time.

♥ If you feel hungry after a meal, wait 20–25 minutes. It takes a while for your brain to tell your stomach that it's full.

♥ Eating slowly will help you feel full quicker.

♥ Weigh yourself only once a week or you may become discouraged.

♥ If you feel depressed or upset, don't grab food—call a friend, listen to music, write in your diary, take a walk, look at a magazine, or visit someone. It works!

♥ Add a half hour of an aerobic activity each day. A few good choices are running, biking, and swimming.

♥ After each week of dieting or each loss of two pounds, reward yourself with something you enjoy—a movie, a book, or some favorite activity (but not extra food).

♥ Write a letter to get your mind off food.

♥ When you have reached your ideal weight, stop. More dieting is unhealthy.

♥ Try to include more carbohydrates, such as pasta, in your diet. They are less fattening than other foods and provide an excellent source of energy.

♥ Keep a supply of low-calorie snacks on hand, such as the ones I've listed in this chapter. Munch on these when you feel hungry.

♥ If you have any questions about your weight or other diet and nutrition concerns, the dietitian at any hospital in your area will always be glad to help you. Give them a call.

A busy schedule and the availability of fast food restaurants sometimes causes us to consume lots of calories with very few nutrients. Many of us neglect to include the five food groups into our daily diet.

Two common problems amongst teens today are filling up with sugary foods and drinks, and dieting so severely that their health is at risk. This can lead to two very serious eating disorders, anorexia and bulimia.

What Are Anorexia And Bulimia?

Anorexia and bulimia are two eating disorders seen mostly amongst teenage girls and young women.

During puberty, girls your age are supposed to put on weight. You're growing taller and your body is getting bigger. This weight gain does not happen overnight. It may take several years to accumulate a few pounds. You may gain more weight one year than another. It depends on how much you grow each year. Your body is also preparing itself for motherhood. Your breasts are developing and you've noticed more weight gain around your waistline and hips.

However, girls often become depressed and worried because they see themselves gaining weight. After all, magazines and television show beautiful females who are thin and tall. Most girls try to look like this, not realizing that it is impossible.

The size and shape of an individual has a lot to do with heredity. If your mom, dad, or grandmother were short, chances are you will be, too. If they have broad shoulders, you may develop these along with their breast and foot size.

Many girls refuse to accept their weight and appearance. They want to look beautiful and thin. As a matter of fact, most girls are concerned about this when they reach your age.

Because of the many visual images of thinness from the media, girls start thinking that if they aren't thin and beautiful (according to how they see themselves), they must start to look for ways to achieve the look they desire.

They're pressured to buy "Barbie" dolls and believe in the perfect "Barbie" image. Clothes, make-up, material items, and glamour are portrayed as the goal for a dream come true. Barbie has perfect hair, a perfect figure, car, house, and of course, the perfect boyfriend. Pre-teen girls think that they will be happy if their life is like Barbie's. As they enter their teen years they continue to think about the "Barbie" image.

They bombard cosmetic counters, thinking more expensive products will make them more beautiful. They also buy or investigate a diet plan of some sort to help them drop the most pounds possible in the least amount of days.

Instead of talking with other girls with the same concern, or their parents, counselor, or doctor, they decide to change their appearance on their own. At this point they don't realize how dangerous this can be. All they want is to look thin and beautiful.

They now begin their diet by practically starving themselves, living on only a few calories a day. When this seems to work, they continue to eat less and less in order to lose more weight. This is called anorexia nervosa.

Signs of Anorexia Nervosa

- Continual dieting even if less than normal weight.
- Loss of menstrual periods.
- Thinking about food and calories a lot of the time, eating very little.
- Refusing to gain weight even when suggested by a physician.
- Failure to gain weight during the growth period.
- No matter how much weight they lose, they still see themselves as being fat.
- Excessive exercising.
- Hair that looks dull, nails that look yellow, overall unhealthy appearance.

Bulimia

This is another very serious eating disorder. It's when girls eat a large quantity of food and then make themselves throw up. Sometimes they may even use laxatives in order to cause diarrhea or diuretics to rid themselves of excess water. They feel guilty over the amount of food they've eaten, thinking that they will gain more weight. So they make themselves throw up to get rid of the food. They don't realize that this causes stress and guilt because of the bulimic behavior—not to mention health hazards that can occur like loss of too much water in the body, heart or kidney damage, tooth and gum damage, and also bowel and stomach problems.

Signs of Bulimia

♥ Using laxatives or diuretics to lose weight.

♥ Self-induced vomiting.

♥ Excessive fear of gaining weight.

How serious anorexia and bulimia are depends on how long the girl has had the condition. Some girls continue the behavior for years. After a period of time, damage has been done to the internal organs that can be difficult to reverse. Bulimia seems to be somewhat worse because misuse of laxatives can cause serious damage to internal organs. If either condition has progressed too far, the girl could even die, because it then becomes too late to reverse the problem. The damage is permanent.

Who Is At Risk?

Eating disorders can happen to anyone; even boys are known to have them. But as I said earlier, girls and young women comprise 90 percent of the population who suffer with these disorders.

Anorexia And Bulimia Can Start For A Variety Of Reasons

♥ There may be pressure from people around you to look skinny. Girls you associate with may tell you people will like you better if you're thin.

♥ Your self-esteem may be low or you feel down or alone. You think that not eating will make you thin and then people will notice you and give you more attention.

♥ Kids at school make comments about your weight. You're self-conscious so you go on a very low calorie diet—not knowing you're hurting your body.

♥ You're feeling pressure from your parents because they expect you to get straight A's, plus have perfect behavior and an excellent appearance. If you don't eat they may feel sorry for you and back off.

Whatever the reason may be, it's important that you become aware of how dangerous these eating disorders are. Think about what it would be like with needles feeding you because your internal organs are damaged.

If you're thinking about starving yourself or dieting because you're emotionally upset or unhappy, find someone to talk to about it. A school counselor or teacher can help you get started. You can also call your family doctor. If she thinks you are overweight, she will recommend a healthy diet for you. It will make you feel a lot better knowing you've had advice from a professional. Years later you'll thank yourself for keeping your body and mind healthy and alive during your growing years.

Reread Chapter One of this book, "Feeling Good About Yourself." An eating disorder is not the answer to raising your self-esteem. If you like yourself, you will appreciate and take care of the body you were born with. As I mentioned, there are other ways to deal with your problems.

If you believe you are overweight, ask your doctor to help you decide on an eating plan the next time you go in for a checkup. You may see yourself as being too fat when you're really not. The reassurance and advice of a doctor can help you maintain your proper weight.

It may also be a good idea to examine your weekly exercise schedule. Keeping your weight down will be much easier if you're active. Ride a bike, take walks, sign up for a sport or activity in your school or community. Not only will you keep your weight down, but you will meet new young people as well.

Notes

Notes

CHAPTER 11

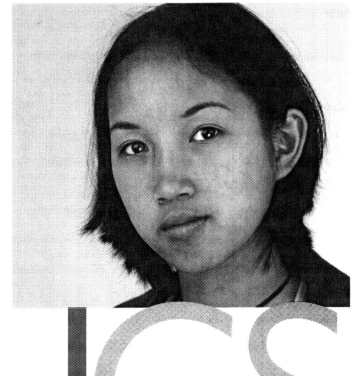

DRUGS

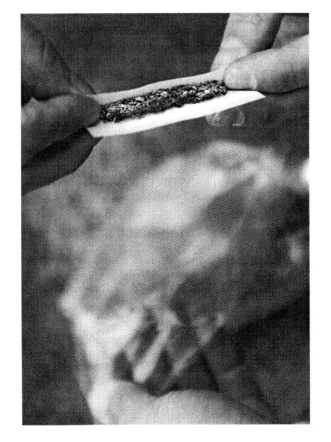

Pressure to take drugs is everywhere. You may be asked to use drugs because the group you hang around with uses them. If you don't go along, others may tease you or call you names or even start untrue rumors about you. If you belong to a gang, they may even try to hurt you if you don't say "yes."

After you read this chapter, you'll ask yourself "Why would anyone want to destroy her mind and body with drugs?" You'll also feel more like saying no because if you like yourself and who you are, you will want to keep yourself healthy and happy. A little harassment from peers is nothing compared to the consequences you'll live with if you use drugs.

Drugs And Their Side Effects

Drugs which are not prescribed by a doctor or

sold in stores are illegal. Most of these are addictive and extremely dangerous.

Drugs may make you feel good for a short time, but are the side effects and consequences worth it?

Marijuana and hashish: These are smoked like tobacco and make the user feel "high." They can become psychologically addictive, and people who use them may go on to use more dangerous drugs. *Side effects:* More dangerous than cigarettes if used regularly. Users may have higher risk of chronic bronchitis, chest colds, and coughing. It also slows the body's ability to fight off germs. Some studies even show that heavy use will disrupt hormone production in men and women. Heavy use can cause irregular menstrual cycles. Use while pregnant can lead to premature birth. Some people feel a panic reaction and feel they are losing control when using the drug. They have trouble remembering things and experience tremors, sweating, irritability, and sleep disturbances.

Amphetamines: These are often known as "uppers" or "speed," and come in tablet or capsule form. They can become addictive and sometimes lead to other hard drug use. *Side effects:* Users may experience a rise in blood pressure and heart rate, and also a decrease in appetite. You may also experience dizziness, headaches, a dry mouth, anxiety and sleeplessness. The user becomes anxious, moody, and restless.

Barbiturates: These are also known as "downers" or sedatives because they make the user relaxed, tired, or sleepy. *Side effects:* Too much of this drug can cause drowsiness and confusion. Mixing this drug with alcohol may be deadly.

Cocaine and crack: This is a dangerous, addictive drug that is sniffed through the nose (snorted) or sometimes injected with a needle like a shot. Crack is a form of cocaine that is smoked. *Side effects:* Can cause an increase in heart rate and reduce blood supply to the heart which can lead to blood clots. It can also lead to heart attacks or irregular heartbeats. Overdose can cause coma and death.

Heroin: This is an extremely harmful and addictive drug that is injected with a needle into a vein. Not used as often as other types of drugs. *Side effects:* Can cause convulsions and coma. Because it's injected with a needle, the user is also at risk for getting the AIDS virus.

PCP "Angel Dust": Makes you high and produces a feeling of emptiness. *Side effects:* A very dangerous drug that causes confusion and bizarre behavior, with a rise in blood pressure, which could lead to death. This drug causes one to do crazy, dangerous things like walking off balconies.

LSD: This drug was used more many years ago. It was used in sugar cubes or in powder form.

People used it to escape into daydreams as they became high. *Side effects:* Users may experience nightmares and increased pulse and respiration rates. It can also cause paranoia and hallucinations. Paranoia is a state in which a person thinks that others are out to get them. Hallucinations are feeling, seeing, or hearing things that aren't there. These side effects can last for many years.

NOTE: Research shows that when women are on drugs while pregnant, their chances of producing abnormal babies is very high. These are babies that are born with something wrong with them because the mother was using drugs.

Why Kids Use Drugs

Drugs, like alcohol and cigarettes, are tried for many reasons.
1. They may be easily obtained from friends and everybody seems to be trying them.
2. Your friends may convince you that drugs will ease your problems.
3. Drugs may seem like an escape from pressure at school or at home.
4. Your parents may be using them.
5. You want to see what it feels like when you're on drugs.

Once again, I must repeat myself and say, "Do not hurt your body. When you take drugs, this is what you are doing. Don't! It's dangerous and deadly."

You will be faced with many difficult decisions as you grow older. Even as an adult, you will have difficult decisions to make. However, you do not need to take drugs to get through an uneasy time in your life.

Maybe your parents are divorcing, or someone close to you has died. You are lonely and depressed because you don't have friends. Or, maybe you're depressed a lot and you don't know why. You may even take drugs just because it gives you something to do or because you have free time on your hands.

Often, we take the easy way out, using drugs to escape from problems rather than facing them. Drugs numb your feelings only for a short time. When they wear off, your problems will still be there. That's why it's better to solve them in a healthful way. It's the best protection you can give yourself.

How Drugs Affect Our Lives And The Lives Of Others

Taking drugs means you need money to pay for them. When kids don't have enough, they borrow from friends without paying them back. They may have to steal from parents or other family members. As their drug problem becomes worse, they become very rude to people, often pushing them around and making unreasonable demands. This is because the drug has worn off and they have mood swings until they fill themselves up once again.

I remember a family with a boy who was on drugs. His mother spent hours up at night worrying about where he was. When he was home she couldn't talk with him because he wasn't thinking straight because of the drugs. He couldn't answer her questions or take care of himself conscientiously. His thinking was very confused, and his parents weren't sure what was really wrong with him.

This went on for a long period of time. Finally he was arrested and put in jail. He later received treatment, but people were always suspicious when the question of drugs came up. Later on, after the boy married and started a life of his own, people who knew him still suspected he was using drugs. I don't know if he will ever erase his drug record. He may have to live with it forever. However, people can make a better life for themselves in spite of past drug use.

Reasonable Decision Making

The decision not to take drugs is a smart one, but how do you do it? You may feel like your friends won't accept you if you say no. You'd be surprised. Not everyone at school takes drugs. According to statistics, most people don't. Today more and more teens are proud to say they are substance-free. Taking care of your body and staying healthy are "In." They are also not harassed because of it, because they have a way of avoiding these people politely and quickly. Don't get mad and make a scene if someone approaches you. Just say no politely, don't offer a reason, and go about your business.

If you want to give a reason, some you might use are:

1. My parents will ground me forever.
2. I'm allergic to drugs.
3. Remember: Just say no.
4. I've tried it and don't like it.
5. It's not for me.
6. I'm on my way to the gym in a few hours.

Having a drug problem isn't the end of the world. Many people understand what you're going through. Once again, consider asking for help from parents, your school counselor, a relative, family doctor, or your teacher. No one needs to know except the people you ask to help you. If you still can't get up enough nerve to ask any of the above, but still want help, call the help hotline in back of this book. The number is toll free and no one on the other end will know you.

Some points to remember:

1. Take it one day at a time. You can't handle, "How will I feel next week?" Concentrate on

the moment and day you're going through at the present time.

2. Set a reasonable goal for yourself and reward yourself for hanging in there.

Alcohol

Alcohol use amongst teens today is probably a greater concern than drug use. Alcohol use is especially high for teens between the ages of 14 and 17. Even at this early age, teens begin to have alcohol problems. Males are more susceptible abusing alcohol than females, but many girls do have problems with alcohol.

Like drugs, people drink for either social reasons or to escape from problems. They may also drink because their friends are doing it.

Some studies show that children of alcoholic parents are more likely to drink than children of non-alcoholics. There seems to be a genetic link of some kind. Keep this in mind because you may have children someday.

Women and teens who weigh less are also affected by a smaller amount of alcohol than a heavier male. One or two drinks may make them feel like you've had ten.

Reasons People Drink

1. To escape from problems.
2. Other people are drinking.
3. It's easy to get.
4. Something to do during spare time.

Suicide rates are higher amongst people who are heavy alcohol users, and so are deaths caused by accidents. Forty-four percent of automobile accident deaths caused by drinking occur amongst teens between the ages of 16 to 25. This is one reason the penalty for drinking and driving is serious. People don't realize how they not only endanger their own lives, but the lives of others as well.

Drinking can also affect an unborn baby through a condition called "Fetal Alcohol Syndrome" (FAS). Drinking while pregnant can cause the baby to be mentally retarded or have heart or other body defects. Studies even show that if a man drinks during the month before conception it can lower the birth weight of the baby. You can understand how serious drinking can be, not just for you, but for your unborn baby as well.

Side effects: Poor eating habits may develop, fatigue (a feeling of tiredness), respiratory problems, mood changes, and sleep disorders.

NOTE: Combining drugs and alcohol is called potentiation or synergism. The more you take, the more your body will need—and after being hooked, it's extremely difficult to stop without professional help. You may suffer shaking, depression, sweating, and a rapid pulse. If this is happening to you, get help immediately. Your condition is already very serious and you don't want it to get worse.

Smoking

Smoking has been around for a very long time. Years ago people had a cigarette after a meal or while they were sitting around and relaxing.

Since smoking is usually seen amongst adults, young people think that if they start smoking they, too, will feel grown up and more mature. Television commercials and magazine ads are partially responsible for this.

Before the 1960's little was known about the danger of smoking—but not any more. Medical evidence provides the public with facts about how damaging smoking is to our health. Some of the findings reported are:

- ♥ People who smoke have a greater chance of dying from a heart attack and respiratory problems.
- ♥ Smoking causes more wrinkles because the blood vessels constrict.
- ♥ There is a very close relationship between smoking and cancer, and not only lung cancer, but also cancer of the bladder, pancreas, and mouth.
- ♥ Smoking potentially threatens the health of unborn babies. Women should try not to smoke while pregnant.
- ♥ People who smoke are more susceptible to ulcers or stomach problems.

Side Effects: If a person continues to smoke, it may cause chest pains, coughing, respiratory problems, and even death.

Some Things You Can Try Doing
If You Need To Get Your Mind Off Drugs Or Alcohol

- ♥ Call a friend if you feel stressed.
- ♥ Go for a walk, by yourself or with a friend.
- ♥ Watch a movie or video.
- ♥ Go to church.
- ♥ Write down your feelings in a journal.
- ♥ Listen to music while looking at your favorite magazines.
- ♥ Clean out your closet.

Notes

Notes

CHAPTER

12

Love & Sexuality

Love is one of the most important and powerful emotions you'll ever experience. Like plants need sun and water to live and grow, you, like all human beings, need love to live and grow into a healthy, fulfilled person.

The first kind of love you experience is from and for your parents, or the people who are responsible for your upbringing. As you grow older, you'll experience many other kinds of love.

You'll love one friend more than another. On some days you'll love your dog more than you love your mom. You'll love a certain movie or television star, even though you've never met. You'll love broccoli and hate ice cream.

I remember one of my first graders one day saying to me, "Mrs. Wanner, I love you—in God's way." So you see, there are many different ways that you will love and be loved.

As you grow older, you'll find yourself becoming more attached to one person who makes you feel very special. Your body will feel excited and you'll think about and want to be with that person a lot. This may begin as a close friendship which turns into a loving relationship, or "falling in love." When you love another in this special way you feel a need for acceptance, understanding, caring, and physical closeness.

However, when you and the other person are in love, you must never be pressured into thinking that you must have sex in order to stay in love. Sexual intercourse is not for kids.

There is a lot of pressure among teens today when the subject of sex comes up. You may be asked to have sex because everyone else is doing it or because your boyfriend wants you to. Don't let anyone talk you into doing something that you don't believe in or that you don't want to do. At some time, when you're with someone you like, your body will begin to feel physically ready for sexual intercourse. This doesn't mean you should have sex. It only means that you're becoming a woman.

If you feel pressured to have sex from a boyfriend, be honest and tell him you're not ready. Then show him other ways to be affectionate so he knows you care for him. Let him know that there are many other things that make you feel close to him and that sex shouldn't be the only thing your relationship is based on. After all, you're a pretty special person who is strong and confident enough to make smart choices. Like I said, saying no is easier than living with the consequences of not saying no.

Ask him to understand your feelings and that if he truly cares for you he'll respect your feelings. Then tell him all the reasons you like being with him and talk about how special he is to you.

Here are some ways to show that you care for him:
- ♥ Hugging
- ♥ Walking and talking together
- ♥ Having lunch
- ♥ Playing cards or board games
- ♥ Making him his favorite food
- ♥ Helping each other with homework
- ♥ Holding hands
- ♥ Going to church together
- ♥ Seeing a movie
- ♥ Checking in with him from time to time to see how he's doing

If this doesn't work and he still continues to pressure you for sex, then he doesn't care enough for you or respect you for who you are. You will then have to choose to continue seeing him or break off the relationship. This can be done in a polite and friendly way. Remember your assertive skills and that your opinion is just as important as another person's. Don't give in to what you're not comfortable with.

Having a sexual relationship is not just a sign of caring. It is a commitment of mind and body. It's giving a very special part of yourself and your life to someone. But it can also lead to some very serious consequences like pregnancy and sexually transmitted diseases (STDs)—even AIDS.

Things some boys might say to try to convince girls to have sex:

- ♥ Don't worry, I know what to do so you won't get pregnant.
- ♥ You can't get pregnant the first time.
- ♥ If I withdraw we don't have to worry.
- ♥ You can't conceive when you're menstruating.
- ♥ You can't get pregnant when you're drunk.
- ♥ If you love me you'll have sex.

Don't believe the above statements or anything else you're not sure of, when someone is pressuring you to have sex. The best way to protect yourself is to educate yourself.

You should discuss any type of birth control with an adult who is knowledgeable about it. This person could be a parent. If you feel uncomfortable discussing this with your parents, you could talk with another adult woman who you think can help you. You can also ask your school nurse.

I realize this is a very sensitive issue and that your parents may not agree with your decisions, but it's always best to be open and honest, especially when your physical and emotional health are at risk.

Your parents and other adults you trust are very concerned about your welfare, and sex is not always an easy subject to talk about. Try to use good listening skills. Hear them out and don't interrupt. Consider their point of view and remember that they're concerned about your well-being and happiness. Talk with them politely and try to understand their reasoning.

How Can I Protect Myself?

The most effective and intelligent way you can protect yourself from peer pressure and false information is to educate yourself.

There are a lot of books on the subject of sexual intercourse. You can check these out at your school or your local public library. You can also buy them in bookstores.

There are also many free community health programs to give you accurate information. Check with your school or public librarian, or call the local Chamber of Commerce for information about such programs.

Because some girls don't have a responsible adult to educate them, or because they haven't been informed through reading, they believe rumors and false statements about sex. And some of these girls, even as young as 13 years old, become pregnant, or infected with a sexually transmitted disease (STD).

Some of the most common sexually transmitted diseases are pubic lice, chlamydia, gonorrhea, syphilis, herpes, and AIDS. Medications are available to cure or help relieve the pain for most of these diseases. For some diseases, such as AIDS, there is no cure. No matter what the disease, if the infected person goes untreated, she can suffer damage to internal organs or even die.

It's important that you protect yourself from sexually transmitted diseases. It's hard to believe that there are more than twenty different kinds, but there are.

STDs can be passed through the penis, anus, vagina, and even the mouth. Blood, semen, saliva, and other body fluids may contain the disease. These diseases can make you very ill and can even cause you to become sterile (unable to have children). Some newborn babies of women with STDs become sick and even die.

If caught early, some sexually transmitted diseases can be cured. Some varieties of genital warts, blisters, and sores cannot be cured, but they can be treated with medication. There is no cure for AIDS; it is a deadly disease.

Remember that the more sexual partners you have the greater the risk of getting one of the diseases. That's why people are encouraged to avoid having sexual intercourse until they choose a permanent partner, who they may marry or spend their life with.

What Are Condoms And Foams, And Why Do We Need To Know About Them?

Condoms are contraceptive devices used by a man. He doesn't need a doctor's prescription to buy them. A condom is rolled onto the penis and used both as a birth control device and to help protect against sexually transmitted diseases.

Some women commonly use contraceptive foams to prevent pregnancy. These products also don't require a prescription. Foams look like whipping cream and are placed inside the vagina to prevent pregnancy. As a method of protection against pregnancy and STDs, doctors very often suggest that a couple use both a condom and foam while having sexual intercourse. *KEEP IN MIND:* Condoms and foams are a safe way to prevent pregnancy and sexually transmitted diseases, but THEY ARE NOT 100 PERCENT EFFECTIVE. Abstinence is the only 100 percent effective method.

What Are Some Other Methods Of Birth Control?

I believe people as young as you shouldn't have sexual intercourse—this is the only sure way of avoiding an unwanted pregnancy or disease. However, if this isn't your choice, and you've made a well-thought-out decision to have sex, you should protect yourself against an unwanted pregnancy. The following methods are among those most common.

1. Birth Control Pills— 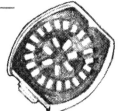 A hormone pill, taken daily, which prevents the ovaries from releasing an egg. These pills must be prescribed by a doctor.

2. The Cervical Cap— This is a soft rubber device that is shaped like a thimble. It is smaller than a diaphragm. Spermicidal jelly or cream is used with it.

3. Condom—  A thin piece of rubber that is slipped over an erect penis before intercourse. Cream or spermicidal foam or jelly is also used.

4. Vaginal Contraceptive Sponge—This sponge can be purchased over-the-counter in most drugstores. It's used by adding water along with spermicide nonoxynol-9.

5. Foams & Chemical Contraceptives—  These are inserted into the vagina like a tampon. This is mostly used along with another type of birth control.

6. Diaphragm—  A soft rubber device shaped like a dome. It must be measured and fit for you by a doctor. To insure maximum protection, your doctor may recommend that you use a diaphragm and your partner use a condom.

7. Norplant—  With this method, a doctor makes a small cut under the skin of a woman's upper arm and inserts six rubber capsules. These capsules release a hormone that stops ovulation.

8. Family Planning—This method requires you to keep track, on a calendar, when you ovulate (when the egg cell inside you is released, making it possible for you to get pregnant). This method is very unreliable, so check with a doctor before trying it.

9. Abstinence—More and more teens today are choosing abstinence as a birth control method. They choose to wait for their life-long partner out of respect and love for that person, and they also don't want to be faced with AIDS.

Abortion

I sincerely hope that you will never have to make this choice. Some girls think it's no big deal to have an abortion, but they have no idea that it's a surgical procedure that often leaves painful emotional scars for months or years. Simply deciding whether or not to have an abortion can be emotionally painful and exhausting. There also may be physical complications, as with any surgical procedure.

If you decide to have sexual intercourse before you are married, I hope you consider a reliable method of birth control. Your physical and emotional health should always be primary concerns. Any of the birth control methods mentioned earlier would be better than having an abortion because you didn't protect yourself.

What Do I Do If I'm Pregnant?

If you know you're pregnant and hadn't planned on it, you will go through a lot of different emotions. You'll experience feelings of anger, shock, fear, sadness, excitement, happiness, and even contentment. The negative feelings may come from thinking about the responsibility of a baby at such a young age. Girls feel happy and excited because they were glad they were able to get pregnant.

There are more unwanted or early pregnancies today than ever before. If this happens to you, don't feel as if you're alone; you're not.

One reaction girls feel when they become pregnant is a feeling of aloneness. They are afraid to tell anyone. They feel their parents will yell at them, kick them out of the house, or punish them forever. It's natural to feel this way. After all, this wasn't supposed to happen.

Right now you need to think about you and the baby. You have a lot of decisions to make—decisions you shouldn't have to make alone. You should let the father of your baby know. His parents should also be informed. Your parents and his may be very supportive and helpful in making a wise decision about the situation.

I know you may think that your parents are the last people you could depend on to help you. It may surprise you to know that many parents faced—or could have been faced—with the same situation you're in now.

Yes, your parents will be shocked and they may even get angry. But after they see how helpless you are their reactions may change. Parents are very concerned for your happiness and well-being. Let them help you. They will eventually find out so you might as well tell them right away and get it over with.

Let's say your parents don't accept your pregnancy and they ask you to leave. You then need to call a friend, neighbor, relative, or adult you trust. Keep calling until you find someone who will help you.

There will be many questions you may need help answering. That's why you should talk with someone about your problem, someone more experienced who can help you make good choices.

Having a baby will change your life forever, no matter how old you are. You will have issues to explore:

- ♥ Do I keep the baby or give it up for adoption?
- ♥ Do I stay in school? If so, how will I care for the baby?
- ♥ How much responsibility does the father have?
- ♥ How do I face kids at school?
- ♥ Will my parents feel uncomfortable having me around their friends?
- ♥ Where will I get the money to take care of the baby without a high school diploma and a job?
- ♥ Will I be willing to stay home and take care of the baby when I'm not in school? Or will I miss my social time with friends?

If you become pregnant and have a child while you are very young, consider what it was like when your parents raised you. Did they give you food, clothes, love, and attention? Did they give you support and understanding throughout your growing years? Then you also need to do the same for your child. It's your responsibility as a parent.

You can see how an unplanned pregnancy can change lives and create problems. The birth of a baby is a miraculous gift. A life should be brought into the world with joy and celebration. I hope when and if you have a baby it is at a time when you're ready to accept the responsibility.

What Is A Crush?

When you have sexual feelings for someone and like being around that person, we call this a crush. People have all different kinds of crushes. Sometimes they have a crush on a teacher, coach, movie star, or a brother's friend. Most of the time crushes don't last very long. Some girls may even have a crush on more than one person at a time. A few girls spend the majority of their time thinking and fantasizing about their crush and forget what's happening around them.

I remember a day when my daughter and her girlfriends were discussing one of their male junior high school teachers. They described him as being handsome, cool, and smart, with a sense of humor. They loved going to his class. All three of them had a crush on him.

Having a crush on your teacher is very normal. After all, you are around him every day. He's intelligent, in control, and comes across as a very caring person. It's easy to start fantasizing about all the things you'd like to do with him.

If your thoughts and feelings are on your mind too much, you'll have trouble studying or remembering what people say to you. You may stop yourself from having fun with other kids. You need to talk with someone about it. Ask your friend, teacher, or school counselor if you can speak with one of them. There may be another reason you're becoming attached to your teacher. Maybe you're not getting enough attention at home or you don't have friends. You see this teacher as someone who gives you attention and spends time talking with you.

It's also normal for girls to feel that a person of the same sex is special and attractive. This may be a female teacher or girlfriend. You may feel a special closeness that you don't feel with anyone else. You may not want to spend time with anyone other than her. There may even be some jealousy if that girlfriend spends more time with other kids.

This feeling passes most of the time. As girls grow older they start developing an attraction for the opposite sex. Yet some girls continue to have feelings of closeness and sexual feelings for other females well into their adult years. This is called homosexuality.

If you have sexual feelings, thoughts, or fantasies about someone of the same sex, consider it very common. It doesn't mean you choose for it to happen.

The same is true for a girl having a crush on her female teacher. She may be someone you respect, admire, is fun to be around, and who might have a lot going for her. You might even hope to be just like her someday.

Sexual feelings about other people are just thoughts and feelings that come and go. They are just there. There isn't any reason to feel guilty about having them.

If you're ever uncomfortable about your feelings and it continues to bother you, try talking with a close adult friend, school counselor, psychologist, or family doctor. Don't think you're the first one who's come to them with this concern.

Can Boys Be Just Friends?

It's more common today for girls and boys to be good buddies. They may never have sexual feelings for each other, but they spend a lot of time together because they have many of the same interests.

When my daughter was a teenager she went out—but with a group of kids. She never went out alone with a boy until her junior year of high school. Most kids don't go out in two's these days. They go out with everyone in their crowd. Some of this has to do with the fact that many of them at this age do not have their driver's license. However, they hang around together because they're friends and they like being together, regardless of their sex.

When Do I Start Dating?

Dating practices—or rules—vary from family to family and country to country. When you will be allowed depends on when your parents allow it. There may be several reasons for their decision: the way they were brought up, their religious beliefs, what other parents are doing in your neighborhood, and whether you live in the city or country. The decision they make should be followed and respected. If you think you should date sooner, share your feelings with them politely and listen to their reasons without interrupting or starting an argument.

The same goes for girls who aren't interested in dating, but their parents encourage them because most other kids your age are. Let your parents know that you don't feel comfortable dating and that you're not ready yet. After your talk, your parents will probably be assured that you're normal, but need to grow up and date only when you feel you're ready.

Dating can help you meet people, form new friendships, and provide a closeness everyone enjoys. What is done on a date is another issue.

I believe that there are fun and healthy dating relationships but there are unhealthy ones, too. When choosing who to date and what to do on your date, consider the following:

Healthy Dates	*Unhealthy Dates*
♥ School socials or sporting events	♥ Drinking and smoking
♥ Going to the movies	♥ Using drugs
♥ Playing board games	♥ Having sex
♥ Watching TV or videos	♥ Violent acts such as hitting or kicking
♥ Walking the mall	♥ Having a lot of kids over when
♥ Skating, swimming, playing tennis	parents are gone

If you get into a situation where unhealthy things are happening while you're on your date, get away. The following are reasons you may use to leave the party or date.

> ♥ Tell him you have to call and check in with your parents.
> ♥ Tell him you forgot your medication at home and you need it as soon as possible.
> ♥ Let him know that you're not feeling well and need to leave.
> ♥ Tell him you don't do that kind of stuff.

You need to once again use your assertive skills and be polite and friendly. You are the only one who can take control of yourself and your actions, not to mention your safety. If things really get bad and you feel like you're in a dangerous situation, go to a neighbor next door for help or call 911 when no one is in the same room. The important thing is to prevent anyone from getting hurt, including you.

Notes

Notes

SCHOOL

While growing up, most of your time will be spent in school. This is probably where you'll make your best friends, learn about your favorite subject, experience most of your inner emotions, notice bodily changes, and tell lots of secrets. Your classmates are people you'll remember forever. You will never see some of them again, but you'll at least exchange Christmas cards every year with others.

It's important that you do what you can to make your school experience as positive as possible. On some days this will be easy. Other kids will make you feel special and accepted, but on other days, no one will want to be around you.

Since I am a teacher, I try to stress the importance of school in learning and preparing for a career. Learning how to function in the world as adults is important, too. However, there are many other things going on in schools today. Kids need to learn social skills as well as academic skills, and this becomes challenging if you aren't knowledgeable and prepared.

The information in this chapter should relieve frustrations that occur at school. However, it's important to remember that situations will arise for which you don't have answers. You will then need to talk with someone. It can be a teacher, social worker, principal, psychologist, or another adult you trust.

How Important Are Good Grades?

You should feel proud of getting good grades. For some, this comes naturally; for others it takes more work.

I cannot stress enough the importance of good grades—not necessarily straight A's, but good grades—doing the best you can.

Good grades can help you feel proud and confident because you've succeeded. Think back when you didn't do so well on a test. You probably felt pretty yucky, huh? You can see how getting good grades can help you feel special and sure of yourself—and ready to try again.

You need a good grade point average if you plan to go to college. Otherwise you may not be

accepted to the college you choose. That's why learning how to study and do well now will make a big difference in your future plans. Learning all you can in high school will help you make important decisions about your college and job plans.

The same goes for your college years. Cramming for tests and passing just to get through school is not wise. Think how much more knowledge you will have when you start your new job someday if you study hard now. You'll keep your job, and be asked to stay with the company longer because you're good at your job, making you a more successful adult. Your success may lead to a managerial position and maybe one day, you'll own your own company.

In the elementary grades both boys and girls appear to like school. They like learning new information, interacting with other students, and being challenged. At this age, boys and girls are fairly equal regarding their academic feelings.

When kids enter junior high, there seems to be quite a change in feelings and attitudes regarding their place in school. For several reasons, some girls' self-esteem becomes low. They may feel guilty or stupid if they fail or if they can't understand what the teacher is saying. They may not raise their hands or offer to participate in discussion groups for fear of looking dumb.

Boys, on the other hand, are seen as being cute and entertaining if they don't know the answer or if they make smart-aleck remarks while in class.

As you grow older, you probably notice that some teachers suggest that you take classes that aren't in math and science. They will assign the required classes and that's it. You're rarely encouraged to take additional classes leading to a math and science related career. But boys are placed in classes where they are encouraged to pursue careers in math and science.

Many parents do not understand how advanced technology has become. They don't know the kinds of skills daughters need to prepare themselves for future careers. So they, along with other adults, do not encourage young girls to become skilled in math and science.

If you plan to pursue a career as a nurse, doctor, biologist, or veterinarian, for example, you will need a good math and science background.

Just think of a time when you visited a doctor and he or she prescribed medicine for you to help you get well. You were probably happy because the doctor helped cure your illness. What if you had been told that he or she didn't know how to help you and sent you away? The doctor would not have a job!

Remember when I told you about the roles women had years ago? (Chapter 2, Assertiveness.) Many women were—and still are—seen as somewhat passive and dependent instead of brainy decision makers. This attitude is slowly changing. It's up to you to choose classes that will help you in your career and not be steered away from classes that are considered to be for boys only.

How many offices and schools and businesses have you seen where there is no computer? Not too many. Even if you decided not to enter college and you worked in a store instead, you would still need math and computer skills.

Teachers, parents, and employers are realizing more and more that girls, too, need a firm foundation in technology in order to function effectively in the modern world.

Where Can I Get Information On What Classes I Need To Help Me Prepare For My Career?

The best place to start is with a school guidance counselor. These professionals have information that can help you decide which courses are best for you. If you don't get the answers you're looking for, call your local community college or university. Tell them you need to talk with someone. They will help you set up an appointment with an advisor, who can lead you in the right direction.

Homework

Most kids do not like homework, but there are not enough hours in a school day to cover all the material you need to know. Homework is also a way to reinforce what you learned that day, because it helps you remember what your teacher presented in class.

The best way to approach homework is to think of it as winning a game like a computer game. Challenge the teacher and the teacher's manual. Show them that you can match the right answers. How exciting to hand in that paper and experience the suspense of waiting for the results. Yes!

How To Take Notes In Class

Learning how to take notes is very important, especially when studying for tests. Often, students write down too much or too little information, making their notes unusable.

Let's look at how you can take notes without becoming frustrated.

1.   Always use lined paper.

2.   Listen carefully to what your teacher is saying. If she or he expresses important information, write it down quickly in a simple sentence.

3.   If she gives facts about the topic, list those, too.

4.   Skip words like "an," "the," and "is," because these take more time to write.

5.   Always ask your teacher to clarify or explain something you don't understand.

6.   Put your notes with other study sheets used for that chapter.

Using Your Notes To Study

1.   Read your notes back to yourself aloud.

2.   If you were in a hurry and didn't get all the information down, finish writing in what you think you need to remember.

3.   Add anything else you forgot to jot down. Underline in another color or use a highlighter to emphasize names, events, etc.

4. Lastly, go over your notes with a friend if possible. You may be able to get a few new ideas from each other.

Tips For Effective Studying

It will be a lot easier for you to get your homework done if you get everything at home set up and ready. Don't expect your parents to do this for you. You may need to ask them for a place to study—a place that's private, where you can set up your homework tools. Your room is probably a good place. If you don't have a desk or table in your room, ask your parents to help you set up something that can stay there permanently.

Once you have a space, ask them to get you a lamp that helps keep your area well lighted. Some kids have a TV and radio in their room. Most of the time, these should be turned off when you're studying. Having the radio on or soft music playing is sometimes helpful to get through your homework, if you're not studying for a test. My daughter seemed to get her homework done more often if she listened to quiet music. Just make sure the radio isn't loud—this isn't a party. No one should be allowed in your homework space. Let your parents know this if you have brothers or sisters.

Now, let's look at a list of homework tools everyone should own.

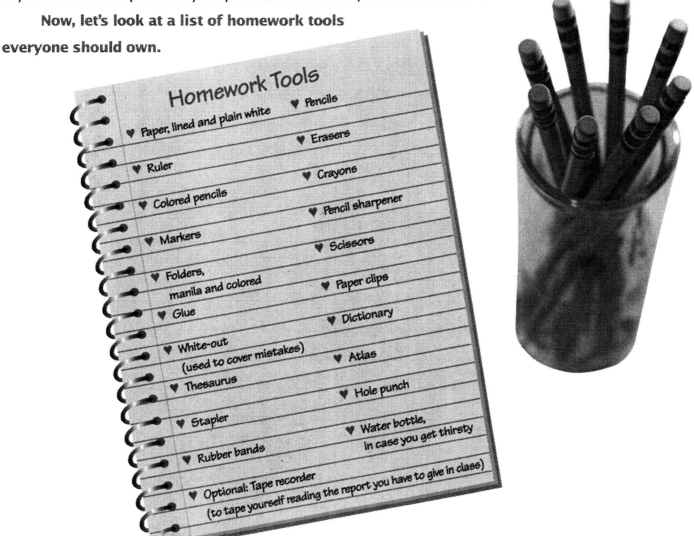

Homework Tools

♥ Paper, lined and plain white ♥ Pencils

♥ Ruler ♥ Erasers

♥ Colored pencils ♥ Crayons

♥ Markers ♥ Pencil sharpener

♥ Folders, manila and colored ♥ Scissors

♥ Glue ♥ Paper clips

♥ White-out (used to cover mistakes) ♥ Dictionary

♥ Thesaurus ♥ Atlas

♥ Stapler ♥ Hole punch

♥ Rubber bands ♥ Water bottle, in case you get thirsty

♥ Optional: Tape recorder (to tape yourself reading the report you have to give in class)

This is how I have my writing area set up. It helps save time because when I need things, I don't have to run for them. I also keep some of my things in little baskets. This keeps my space more organized.

Use your weekly assignment page and write down every daily assignment. You'll also need to decide on the best time to do your homework. Many of my students do their homework right after school or after dinner. That way they have the rest of the evening to relax and enjoy their free time.

As much as possible, try to stick to the same schedule each day. If you need help with your work,

My Homework Schedule

MONDAY   **Reminders**
Subject:
Subject:
Subject:
Subject:
Subject:
Subject:

TUESDAY
Subject:
Subject:
Subject:
Subject:
Subject:
Subject:

WEDNESDAY
Subject:
Subject:
Subject:
Subject:
Subject:
Subject:

ask your parents. If they can't help you, ask your teacher if she can explain things at a convenient time for both of you. Many students have to ask their teachers for outside help. Don't be embarrassed about this.

Your monthly calendar allows you to see ahead the projects that are due so you can prepare in advance. Get into the habit of using a calendar, because you will use one for the rest of your life.

NOTE: You may want to ask your parents to read this chapter. It will give them ideas on how to set up your homework/study area.

For The Week Of: _____

THURSDAY	Reminders
Subject:	
Subject:	
Subject:	
Subject:	
Subject:	
Subject:	

FRIDAY

Subject:
Subject:
Subject:
Subject:
Subject:
Subject:

SATURDAY

SUNDAY

How To Study

I remember when I taught fourth grade. Some of my students had no idea how to study—especially for a test. After I noticed several of them failing, I asked them if they had studied. They said, "yes." I then asked them how they studied. Most of them said they read the material. Well, I realized that it was pretty difficult for kids to pass a test when they had no idea how to study for it.

We began to go over a plan on how to study for a quiz, test, or discussion session.

1. Survey
   - ♥ Look over headings and subheadings.
   - ♥ Read the summary and questions at the end of the chapter.
   - ♥ Look at pictures, cartoons, graphs, or anything that relates to the chapter.
2. Question
   - ♥ Turn your heading into a question and after you read the chapter see if you can answer the question.
3. Read
   - ♥ Read the chapter and concentrate. If you have to, read out loud.
   - ♥ Write down the important things such as people and events—things your teacher may test you on.
   - ♥ One way to remember is to form a word or picture in your mind using the people or events.

For example:

Memorize this to remember the seven continents.	Memorize this to remember four important presidents of the United States.				Memorize this to remember your primary and secondary colors.

A   A
    A
A   N   A
    E
    S
	(1)
	Washington
	(WL)
		(16)
		Lincoln
			(32)
			Roosevelt
			(RK)
				(35)
				Kennedy
					R
					P O
					Y B
					G

4. Recite
   - ♥ Recite to yourself what you read. It may help to look in the mirror while doing this.
   - ♥ Tell yourself about the people or events you'll probably have to know for the test.
5. Review
   - ♥ Look over the headings and subheadings again.
   - ♥ Read summaries and questions.

   NOTE: You can continue to use steps 4 and 5 as often as you like up until it's time to take your test. But don't try to cram too much in all at once. Your mind can only memorize a certain amount of material in one sitting.

I found that once my students learned how to study, they did much better in school and their confidence improved tremendously. It isn't that they couldn't do well, they just didn't know how.

Cheating

There are many reasons kids cheat. They didn't have time to do their homework; they can't get very good grades on their own because they don't study; or, they don't feel confident to try to do well on tests and assignments.

I've known kids who have helped fellow students with homework and some who have gone as far as giving test answers.

If other kids ask you for your answers and use you to cheat, STOP! Tell them you don't feel comfortable doing it and if your parents or teacher found out, you'd get into trouble. Once again, if you think about the consequences it makes it a lot easier to say NO. I would sure hate to have doctors prescribe medicine for me if I knew they cheated their way through medical school. Cheating does not make you smart.

How To Deal Politely With Teachers You Don't Like

Since you spend much of your time in school, it's important that you learn to get along with your teachers. You don't have to be buddies, but you shouldn't be enemies either. For some kids it's easy to get along with the teacher; for others, it's a year to year challenge. Teachers are just like you. They are around a lot of different personalities and can become irritated and short-tempered just like anyone else. They're human.

If you find yourself in a situation where your teacher dislikes you, there are several things you can do.

First of all, think about how you behave in class. Are you constantly talking or bothering other students? Are you always asking unnecessary questions to get attention? Are you wearing clothes that are clean and appropriate? If you can't think of anything that seems to be the problem, ask a couple of good friends in some of the same classes. Tell them how you feel and ask them to be honest about their opinion. Depending on what they say, you can try to change your behavior. Your teachers may not notice the change immediately, but

give them time. After all, you've been acting that way for a while. When your teachers see that you are making a real effort to improve, they will appreciate it and may make an effort to acknowledge your good behavior in a professional way.

Let's say you don't have a clue about why your teachers dislike you. If you continue to feel shunned or neglected, then you may just have to learn to make the best of the situation. If you have this teacher for only one period a day, it will be easier than if you have the same teacher all day, every day.

Sometimes students are picked on for no reason. They may remind the teacher of former students who were a behavior problem. Or their name may be the same as another disliked student. It happens.

Most kids learn to handle these difficulties quite well. However, sometimes a teacher lowers a grade or criticizes a student's work too harshly. This is wrong and it's time for you to do something about it. Talk with your school counselor and definitely make your parents aware of the situation. They can give you advice about improving your relationship with your teacher. If this continues, and I know it's difficult, but your parents need to step in. Your parents might talk with the teacher alone, or you could be there too. Your teacher will then have to justify the grades you were given and the reason for the negative behavior toward you.

At times it's hard to ask your parents to help with a school problem. You must realize, however, that your grades are recorded marks put in your file and follow with you all through school. You deserve to have what you rightfully earned.

Helpful Hints For A Successful School Year

Here are some ways that may help you make your school experience a good one:

1. Come to school prepared.

2. Dress appropriately and make sure you're clean.

3. If you're new at a school, watch other kids for a while to see which ones you think you'd like to get to know.

4. Join in class discussions and use good conversation manners.

5. Stay alert and awake. This means getting enough sleep.

6. Ask for extra help if you need it. Do this politely.

7. Show good manners with your teachers and other students.

8. Keep a notebook with your daily assignments in it, and don't wait until the last minute to do your homework.

9. Don't pass notes. It's a distraction to everyone, and what you write could be read aloud by your teacher.

10. Don't expect the teacher to play favorites with you.

11. Read test instructions carefully. If you're not sure what to do, ask the teacher. Don't forget to check both sides of the paper for test questions.

12. Don't hurry through a test so you're the first one done. If you do finish early, look over your finished work for mistakes.

How Do I Talk With My Teachers?

It's not always easy to talk to teachers if you have a problem. Sometimes you may think they don't care about you or don't have time to listen to you.

If you have teachers who make you feel uncomfortable, give them a chance. They have their own personalities, just as kids do. It takes a little time to get to know them.

If you have something to talk about with your teachers and you don't know how to approach them, write a note to each saying, "Let's talk." Sign your name and put it on their desks. Your teachers can then set up a time to meet with you outside of class.

Having A Part-Time Job

Having an after-school or weekend job is a good way to learn self-confidence, practice decision making skills, learn about careers, and earn some extra money. It allows you to experience the "real world."

However, it should not interfere with your school work. A couple of days a week is more than enough time for you to devote to earning extra money. I know you feel very grownup and responsible by having a job, but your education should come first.

Not having the time to study or do homework because of a job will hurt your grades. If you can't keep up with school work because you're spending too much time working, it's time for you to make some adjustments so this doesn't happen.

Remember when I said that your grades are important—especially if you plan to enter college. The last thing you want to do is sacrifice your future. You can balance your job time, friends, and school by using the calendars in this chapter. Write down how much time you need for homework. Then divide the rest of your time for friends, family, and also just for yourself. When I plan an organized schedule for myself, I get more accomplished than when I don't make a plan. You can do the same!

Notes

CHAPTER

14

CREATIVE & FUN TIMES

We all have times when we like to be alone—
or with others—and just enjoy the world around us.
We play, dream, and create. This is a very special part
of you because it allows you to use your imagination and
find interesting things to do so that you'll
never be bored.

Here are some activities my
students enjoy doing just for fun.

Collecting

My students bring rock collections to
school every year. Others bring bags of trolls,
stamps, coins, and sea shells. Several have even started
spoon collections from each state or country they've visited.

Whatever collection you decide to take up, it will give you something to look forward to. You feel pride and accomplishment. It's also something you will have to look back on to remember your experiences.

Reading

One of the happiest moments for me is when my students and I are reading a wonderful book together. We discuss the characters and compare them with people we know. Some kids even describe what they think the characters might look like in real life.

There is no limit to your imagination when reading. It's even fun to try and predict the outcome or ending and then see how close you are.

Try discussing a book that you and someone else have read. Share feelings about the characters, events, and how you might have ended the story differently. What fun to express your feelings and voice your opinion! The best part is that no one is right or wrong.

Ask a librarian what books are most popular or appropriate for your age. Librarians can help you because they are familiar with most titles. Or, ask a friend, classmate, or teacher what they would suggest. I am always recommending and assigning good reading material to my students. I'm sure your teacher can help you, too.

Strengthen Your Mind

I have students who have a lot of fun memorizing facts about people, places and events. When they present their history report to the class without reading it they show a great deal of pride and accomplishment.

Memorizing exercises help you stay alert and challenge your mind so it will continue to work at a high level.

Some great mind exercises are:

- ♥ Remembering as many names and faces of relatives as possible.
- ♥ Memorize the 50 states and their capital cities.
- ♥ Know the counties in your state.
- ♥ Know who your governor, senators, and state representatives are.
- ♥ Memorize all birthdays in your family.
- ♥ Memorize quotes by famous people.
- ♥ Memorize a new vocabulary word each week, possibly one your teacher gave you in school.
- ♥ Memorize phone numbers of places you call most often.
- ♥ Learn how to clean the humidifier and furnace filter.
- ♥ Learn how to run the lawn mower.
- ♥ Learn how to set up a monthly budget according to the amount of money your family brings home.
- ♥ Check out books from the library on questions and answers about nature. Try to remember as much as you can about what you've read. Tell someone about it.

Sewing

Some of my students sew clothes, which was one of my own favorite pastimes as a young girl. At first it seemed like there was a lot to know, but after I finished my first piece of clothing (a summer robe), I wanted to continue sewing more pieces.

Sewing not only challenges you mentally, it gives you a wonderful feeling of accomplishment. Plus, you get to wear the finished product!

If your mom or a friend can't teach you, have her call some local sewing centers. They have names of people who will sew for others or give sewing lessons.

It's also fun to look through sewing patterns and pick out a simple craft item. You can read the directions and sew the small item on your own. This is a great way to get started if there's no one who can help you.

Create More Space in Your Room

Rearranging your own room, or a room you share with someone else, can be fun. You will be able to find things more quickly and your room will feel new and clean. When your friends come over, you won't need to pile things together in order to make room for them to sit.

Throw out old belongings and make space for the things you use more frequently.

You can use space under your bed, inside your closet, and even behind closet doors.

My daughter and I use many different sizes of baskets and plastic bins to put smaller things in order. The following are a few ways to reorganize:

- ♥ Baskets and plastic bins can be used for hair accessories, books, etc.
- ♥ The space under your bed can be used to store an "under-the-bed box." You can put sweaters or other clothes in it.
- ♥ Hooks on the back of your door can be attached for robes or to hang out your clothes for the next day.
- ♥ A narrow shelf-rack can be placed inside of a closet door for smaller boxes or bottles.
- ♥ A kitchen towel rack with 3 or 4 stems can be hung in your closet for storing bows, hairpieces, and hats.
- ♥ Straw baskets can be used for magazines.
- ♥ A bulletin board is necessary for messages and appointments. It's also fun for hanging some of your favorite photos.
- ♥ One or two large floor pillows would come in handy when friends come over.

Many discount stores have a variety of containers and storage items. You may want to spend a few minutes jotting down some ideas for your "new" room. Then ask your mom or dad to take a look at it with you. You can all discuss your ideas and perhaps come to an agreement on the best way to make more space in your room. Don't be surprised if they love you for trying. Almost all parents are thrilled when kids clean and organize their rooms.

Keeping a Journal

A journal is a perfect way to express your thoughts and feelings. You can write about your happiest and most exciting times or moments when you're feeling sad or angry. Your journal never gives you advice or disagrees. It listens while you write and helps you sort out your feelings.

Many of my students have kept their journals for several years. They've told me how much fun it is to read things that have happened to them in the past. When you're older you may even want to share the journal with your own children.

Starting a journal is simple. Purchase a spiral notebook from a department store. (Any medium or large-sized notebook will do.) You may want one with lines or just blank pages.

Using markers, fabric, construction paper, and other art materials will help make your cover more appealing. Or, you may be satisfied with it the way it is and choose not to decorate it.

On the first page, write the date you are writing. Now, go ahead and write whatever you wish. Try to use complete sentences. They will make more sense and you will be able to understand what you wrote later on, when you look back at your journal.

Drawing

Have you ever seen someone in the park sketching the trees and other surroundings? Drawing is a relaxing way to learn about the details of your environment. You can even frame your drawings and hang them in your bedroom or other places in your home (or give them as gifts!). If you wish to take lessons, call the school administration building and they can give you the name of someone to call.

Painting

This is another relaxing and enjoyable activity. It need not be expensive, either. When you are beginning, buy a box of watercolors and heavy white paper. Go to the park or just stay in your backyard and sketch a simple object. Use your paints to create the look you see.

If you find that painting is something you really enjoy, ask your parents if they know someone who can give you inexpensive painting lessons. You may also try calling your community college and ask if their art department can refer you to someone who gives lessons.

Music Lessons

I remember when my daughter asked to take piano lessons. I was thrilled, but I also knew that buying a piano would be very expensive.

It's best to rent or borrow an instrument at first, until you are sure you want to continue playing. Then your parents won't have to go through the trouble of selling it if you decide piano lessons are not for you.

Many schools offer instrumental music lessons. You will have to rent the clarinet, flute, violin, or trombone on your own. However, this is a good way to experiment with different instruments and find one you enjoy playing.

Another musical instrument is your own voice. You may want to try voice lessons. You can ask a music teacher or check with a music store for possible names. Ask if they have references or names of past customers you could call for information. Most teachers have people you can call. This is much like buying a car or a piece of furniture. You don't buy it unless it seems right for you.

Sports

Swimming

This is one of the best exercises you can choose. You can swim for enjoyment or take lessons and challenge yourself to swim meets or other contests. Knowing how to swim is also a good safety skill when you're near water. Who knows, you could save a life someday!

Biking

Biking helps you feel relaxed. You can enjoy the scenery as you ride, and get great exercise, too. Start by riding for a short while and then increase your time. Eventually your leg muscles will feel firm and you'll be stronger.

Remember to ride safely, look out for traffic, and always wear a helmet. I know people who were hit by a car or truck and are alive and well today because they wore a helmet while riding their bike.

Jumping Rope

This can be done as a warm-up exercise or just for enjoyment—alone or with friends. Don't jump without wearing a good pair of tennis shoes. Like any exercise, start slowly and increase your jumping time as you become stronger.

Tennis and Racquetball

You'll need a court for both of these activities. Tennis is played indoors and outside; racquetball is played indoors so you will have to check with the YMCA or a health club.

Both games are played with other people, so it's a good way to meet new friends. Like many other sports, these exercises increase circulation, reduce stress, tone muscles, increase your energy level, and are great for heart and lungs.

Walking

Walking is an exercise that can be done alone or

with others. It's easy, cheap, and a good way to shape your body. Walking burns calories, tones muscles, improves circulation, relieves stress, and increases energy levels. In addition to improving your posture, it also tones the legs and strengthens muscles in your lower abdomen.

If you walk alone, you may want to wear earphones and take your radio along.

Do a few stretching exercises before you start your walk. Start out slowly and increase your walk time each week. Set a goal of walking a mile or two every few days. Increase your distance as you become stronger.

Golf

Early morning golfing is peaceful and relaxing. This sport will help you work on body balance and concentration. Start with lessons, if possible. This will eliminate frustrations, such as how to stand or how to hold the golf club.

Basketball

This is another great sport that will help you stay in shape while meeting people. You may have a basketball hoop in your own driveway. If not, churches and schools have facilities that are open, with permission, to the public. Your parents, teachers, or the school P.E. teacher may be able to give you helpful suggestions on where to play.

Skiing

Whether you downhill or cross-country ski, the scenery provides memories you will keep for a lifetime. The quiet sounds within, and the blanket-covered hills, make you feel like you're in a different world. Skiing helps you appreciate our world's true beauty.

I recommend lessons for beginning skiers. Otherwise you will become very frustrated as you try to figure out what to do.

Skiing is especially good for your lower body. It also helps with balance and makes your legs stronger.

Lifting Weights

Starting a weight lifting program will give you more strength and body definition. It conditions muscles and helps you concentrate. Girls think that if they lift weights, it will give them larger muscles.

This is not true. It defines or shows the muscle better, but it doesn't make it bigger.

Before starting a weight lifting program, talk with someone who trains or works in a gym. That way you can decide if that's what you want to do.

Throwing a Party

Some of my students say that the best parties are those planned almost on the spur of the moment. Most of your friends are probably ready for a party anytime.

A few hints for planning a party:

1. Decide what kind of party you want to have: a pizza party, a slumber party, a game party, or whatever. Make arrangements with your family so you can have privacy during your party.

2. Make your own invitations in the shape of a pizza, a mask, a puzzle, a hat, or a cartoon. Include the date, time, place, and occasion on the invitation.

3. Decide on decorations. You can buy them or make your own.

4. Use your imagination! Keep in mind the types of friends attending your party. What are their likes and dislikes?

5. Before your guests arrive, prepare your games, puzzles, cassettes, or whatever entertainment you have planned.

6. If you're planning a pizza or popcorn party, you may want to have some favorite sodas on hand.

7. If you're throwing a birthday or Valentine party, fix a pink heart-shaped cake decorated with fresh strawberries.

8. Make sure you greet your guests when they arrive and see them to the door when they leave.

Two Great Punch Recipes

Party Punch

      3 6-oz. cans frozen lemonade

      1 pkg. frozen strawberries, thawed

      1 qt. ginger ale

      Ice

Dilute lemonade according to directions; pour into punch bowl. Stir in strawberries.
Add ginger ale and ice before serving.

Hot Mulled Cider

      1 pint bottle cranberry juice

      2 1-quart bottles apple juice

      1/2 cup brown sugar

      1/2 tsp. salt

      4 cinnamon sticks

Pour fruit juices into 30–36 cup coffeemaker. Place remaining ingredients in basket.
Plug in coffeemaker and perk. When cider is done perking, remove basket assembly. Serve
hot. Makes 40 punch-cup servings.

Notes

SHARING
&CARING

At the beginning of this book I mentioned how important values and family beliefs are. They help you make choices and important decisions that are right for you.

Well, your religious beliefs are part of those values. While growing up you will probably be taught religious traditions used in your home. It's important that you honor and respect them. They help you understand what's right and wrong, what's good and bad, and what it means to get along with other people.

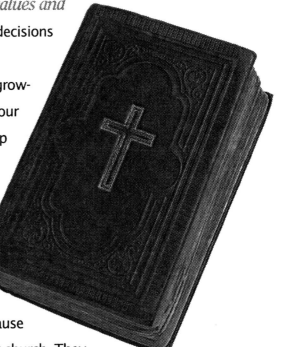

You will notice that your religion might be different than someone else's. That's okay. Within their religion, they're still learning values and beliefs which will help them throughout life.

I know people who have changed religions frequently because they weren't happy with some of the teachings of that particular church. They bounce around from one church to the next, hoping to find a situation that makes everything perfect for them. It's common for people to question or disagree. Most people will not find a religion that fits perfectly with their beliefs and lifestyle. Roaming from one faith to another will most likely cause you just a lot of frustrations.

If you are satisfied with most of the teachings of your religion, you should make an effort to accept the things you cannot change. Try to change your negative attitude by finding a positive reason for the rules of your church or temple. Like I said earlier, you'd be surprised how well it works. A positive mind can be very powerful.

Every so often you hear people talking against religion. Most of the time it's not religion they're angry with. They aren't feeling good about themselves, so they blame religion or God for their problems. If they tried to improve parts of their lives they were unhappy with, chances are they would enjoy their religion much more. Also, I believe that when there are hard times in your life, a place of worship is one place that can help you think through problems.

Besides worshipping in a church or temple and following your values and beliefs, there are other ways that you can show your concern and love for the world, and for the people in it.

Volunteer Work

Volunteering your time for some community service gives you a wonderful sense of belonging to that community. It also helps you become knowledgeable about what's going on around you. Working together with people in your community is an important part of caring for people and helping create change to improve things.

Some ways you can do this are:

♥ Read to young children in the pediatric ward of a hospital.
♥ Spend time helping an older person.
♥ Play with someone who doesn't have any friends.
♥ Help your neighbors with chores if they are sick or elderly.
♥ Ask your parents if you can take a warm casserole dish to a needy person.
♥ Make a surprise Christmas basket and leave it on a poor family's doorstep. Ring the doorbell and run and hide.
♥ Use your allowance money to take a younger child to the movies.
♥ Give your outgrown clothes to someone who needs them.

♥ Offer to read stories to young children in the library.

♥ Call some friends to help you pick up garbage around your neighborhood.

♥ Take stationery and stamps to an older person.

♥ Draw a picture or write a poem for an elderly person. Your works of art will be on their refrigerator forever!

♥ Ask an older person to show you pictures or things about themselves when they were younger.

♥ Volunteer for your church, temple, or school.

You may be able to think of more. A good way to start is to think of someone who needs cheering up or support in some way. Then decide what you can do to help.

In addition to helping people through volunteer work, there are also many benefits for you.

♥ You will probably learn about some history from an elderly person.

♥ Your self-confidence will improve because you are being responsible.

♥ You will be seen as a dependable, conscientious young teen by neighbors and people you know.

♥ It will teach you to appreciate your life when you see how someone less fortunate than you lives.

♥ You will help boost someone else's self-esteem.

♥ Staying busy will keep you from getting bored.

♥ It's fun playing Santa!

Volunteer Your Way To A Career

I don't think girls realize how volunteer work can help them prepare for a career. Any type of work experience—even volunteer—will help you obtain a job in that field. You will also make contacts and learn specialized information that will be valuable in the future.

Think of a career you wish to pursue. Now think of some way you could help in that area and at the same time gain information and experience in that work.

Let's look at a few examples to help you plan your own.

Career	Way to Volunteer
Veterinarian	Help clean up office after hours
Teacher	Put away books or help staple and check papers after school
Marine biologist	Offer to help put pet supplies on shelves or clean cages
Secretary	Ask to answer phone or staple papers on off hours
Nurse	Read to kids in hospital
Travel agent	Ask if you can unpack and display travel information

These are only a few of the many ways you can educate yourself through volunteer work.

If you're not sure what you can do, ask the people you wish to work with what they suggest. They may have tons of little chores they don't have time for. If one place turns you down, go to another. Don't give up. Politely thank them and give them your phone number. You'd be surprised. One day they may not need anyone, another day they may be swamped with extra chores they could use help with.

Our Environment

Our environment is important, too. Our air, water, animals, and plants are all constant reminders to us that we need to do our part to save the earth. We may think we need to do this because people around us are talking about it or it's just a fad. But there's more to it than that.

Our earth has different needs today. We accumulate more garbage than we did years ago and we need to plant more trees to help bring oxygen to the atmosphere. It's important that we each do our part in order to keep the natural balance of nature, especially because our population is growing.

When I was a young girl, spending time outdoors was one of my favorite activities. We didn't watch a lot of television or have video games and malls, so my brothers and sisters and I would play softball, climb trees, build snow houses, and perform for a neighborhood talent show. You can create your own activities.

Take some time for yourself and appreciate the earth, your home:

- ♥ Sit in a park and watch the birds.
- ♥ Listen to the leaves rustle on a breezy day.
- ♥ Lie in the grass and watch the clouds move (a favorite of everyone's).
- ♥ Close your eyes and listen to the wind.
- ♥ Look into the night sky and find the constellations, such as the Big and Little Dippers.
- ♥ Watch the moon and its changes.
- ♥ Watch a flower or plant grow.
- ♥ Write down what you notice each time a season changes.
- ♥ Walk in the rain.
- ♥ Look for a rainbow after the rain.
- ♥ Read about thunder and lightning and why we have them during a rainstorm.
- ♥ Plant a small garden, if you have space in your backyard.
- ♥ Pay attention to the insects and small animals that you see in nature. Learn their names and habits.

We become so involved with what needs to be done that we sometimes forget our real home, our world. Like our faith and our community, our earth is a reminder of who we are and what our purpose is in life.

Notes

CHAPTER 16

My Future

Look around you. How many people do you know who are satisfied with their job? More and more people today are not happy with their chosen career. They spend thousands of hours over a lifetime doing something they dislike. What a waste! Their life would be so much more satisfying if they were doing what they really wanted to.

There are several reasons why people don't fit with the careers they're in. They may have taken the job because:

1. Their parents own the store so they feel pressured to carry through with the family business name.
2. Someone once told them they would be good in that particular skill.
3. The salary is high.
4. The job is close to where they live.
5. The pay isn't high, but the benefits are good.
6. The job was all they could get without a college education.
7. It was the first company that offered them a position.
8. Their office was close to relatives.

The list goes on and on. The sad thing is that they are making choices based on reasons that are not helping them become happy and satisfied individuals.

Some people were never told how to set goals based on their interests. They were never given information about choosing a career that was best for them.

As a result, they find a job and become very frustrated because it's not what they wanted. The longer they stay with it, the harder it becomes to make a change. They may get along with their coworkers most of the time, and after all, it's money they know they can depend on in order to make a living. If they leave, they may not like their new job as well and they may not make as much money.

You can also see how easy it is to talk yourself into keeping a job you don't like rather than taking the time to look for one you'd enjoy more. Taking that risk is very hard for most people.

How Do I Choose A Career?

Finding the ideal career is not always easy, but it can be done. The time you put into preparing for your career will benefit you for a lifetime and will help you become happier with your future.

Most of us have some kind of an idea or picture in our minds of what we see ourselves doing when we grow up. In order to choose the career that is best for you, it is helpful to know what kind of people you might like to work with, the environment you'd like to be in, and the skills needed for your new job. You might also consider how much time you want to spend with your family and if you like working days or nights.

Let's begin by jotting down ideas.

My Ideal Job Survey

Check those most important to you.

A.   I would like to work:

_____	1. Indoors
_____	2. Outdoors
_____	3. With a few people in a small office
_____	4. With many people in a large office
_____	5. For a small business
_____	6. For a large company
_____	7. For a company that requires traveling
_____	8. For a company that does not require travel
_____	9. Travel some
_____	10. In a pleasant, well decorated office
_____	11. Other: _____

B. Kinds of people I would like to work with:

_____ 1. Customers
_____ 2. Several bosses
_____ 3. Clients
_____ 4. Mostly one boss, generally coworkers
_____ 5. Younger people
_____ 6. Other: _____

C. My values:

_____ 1. Don't want to work on my Sabbath
_____ 2. Want to take off for family activities if needed
_____ 3. If I work late, I wish to work at home
_____ 4. Working any time is fine
_____ 5. Other: _____

D. Salary and benefits:

_____ 1. Start at a minimum of $20,000
_____ 2. Health and/or dental insurance
_____ 3. Vacations
_____ 4. Recognition for high sales
_____ 5. Bonus and raise for good performance
_____ 6. Other: _____

E. Skills:

_____ 1. Like working with figures/computer
_____ 2. Like secretarial work/typing
_____ 3. Want to make decisions/work on a team
_____ 4. Speaking in front of people
_____ 5. Like reading and writing
_____ 6. Other: _____

Now that you have listed characteristics about your future job, let's use the information to match your career with what your likes and dislikes are.

Example: **Job:** Teacher

A. I would like to work: indoors and not travel
B. Kinds of people I would work with: younger people
C. Values: not work on Saturday or Sunday
D. Salary and benefits: $20,000
E. Skills: making decisions and speaking in front of people

(Use the chart provided for you in this chapter.)

If you chose teaching for your career, your answers would probably look like the above. If not, then you would list a different job title and see if that one matches. If it doesn't, keep trying until you find one that does.

Matching My Job Survey With A Career

Job: _____

A. I would like to work: _____

_____

B. Kinds of people I would like to work with: _____

_____

C. Values: _____

_____

D. Salary and benefits: _____

_____

E. Skills: _____

_____

You may find that more than one career fits your job survey. This is fine. It just means that as you grow older, you have the time to look at several options. If you narrow your interests down now, your choices won't seem so overwhelming later.

I mentioned earlier in this book how different women's roles were years ago. Certain jobs were considered "man's work" such as law, being a firefighter, architect, or police officer. Positive changes have occurred over the years and women are entering careers now they never dreamed of before.

You're probably wondering why women should consider careers that were held by men in the past. Well, first of all, many of these jobs pay more. If you're going to work in order to support yourself and have enough money for the kind of lifestyle you lead, then a good salary is very important.

Some people have two or more jobs in order to pay their bills and make ends meet. A college education and a good salary would enable them to work only one job. They would also feel more confident if they were prepared and educated for the position.

Another reason to consider looking into "men's jobs" is that you may be very talented and skilled in that particular area. For instance, I know many women who enjoy math and computers. They should have the opportunity to work in those fields. After all, if that's what they like doing, why shouldn't they spend their working hours in jobs they're good at, while making a good salary, too?

When you think about the amount of time you will spend on your job and the bills you will have to keep up with when you're on your own, consider careers that you'll be good at and enjoy, too.

I've told you that some school advisors have a tendency to recommend math, science, or computer courses to the boys. I also said that they most likely will encourage girls to sign up for English, home economics, or literature classes.

Don't agree, if you are interested in subjects they're not recommending. Use your assertive skills, be polite, and express your true feelings. Ask for the courses you want. Don't be pressured into taking classes that won't help you reach your goals.

On the other hand, more advisors are listening to young girls talk about their job interests, and we hope this trend continues.

Below are math requirements for many colleges. Consider them when setting goals for the future. Good math skills are essential for almost every job today. Also, many colleges will not accept you without a good math background. If you enter a math or science-related field, math requirements will include:

Post High School	Two Year College	Four Year College
Algebra, Geometry, Shop, Math	Algebra, Calculus, Statistics	Advanced Calculus, Modern Algebra, Statistics

How Much Money Do I Need To Make A Living?

Having your own job means paying your rent, and having money for groceries, utilities, clothes, medical expenses, and entertainment. It also means planning a budget and sticking to it.

First you need to know how much money you have to spend and then know what your living expenses are. The sample budget below may give you an idea of how you can plan yours.

Monthly Budget

Married with no children in a city of about 50,000

Rent and utilities	$500	Entertainment	80
Car payment	280	Car insurance and maintenance	70
Health insurance, medical and dental bills	230	Gas	70
Groceries	200	Dry cleaning	30
Clothing	150	Savings	50
Eating out	100	Miscellaneous	50
		TOTAL	**$1,810**

Living expenses like those above would require this amount of money per month for you to live on—after taxes are taken out of your paycheck. Knowing how much a job pays and how much money you need helps when you're deciding on a career.

Now take a look at the following jobs and their average annual salaries—before taxes are taken out. Add up what your monthly living expenses might be. Deduct this from your yearly take-home pay. You will then be able to determine whether the job you choose will be enough income for you to live on.

Example: Money needed to live per month	$ 1,810
	x 12
Take-home pay for a year after taxes are deducted	$ 21,720

Look at the following occupations and choose one that you are interested in. Have your parents, teacher, or another adult help you decide how much money is deducted for taxes. The percentage varies depending on where you live and how much money you make, but probably at least 20% of your salary will be taken out right away. Using the leftover money, write down your expenses and see if your take-home salary is enough to pay your bills. This is not only good practice, but is fun to do.

My Monthly Budget

Rent and utilities	_____
Car payment	_____
Health insurance, medical and dental bills	_____
Groceries	_____
Clothing	_____
Eating out	_____
Entertainment	_____
Car insurance and maintenance	_____
Gas	_____
Dry cleaning	_____
Savings	_____
Miscellaneous	_____
TOTAL	_____
Monthly Check	_____
Extra to put into savings	_____

Average Annual Starting And Overall Median Salaries

(Occupational Outlook Handbook, 1996–97 Edition)	Starting	Median
Air Traffic Controller	$22,700	$59,800
Aircraft Pilot (Major Airline)	$27,900	$81,000
Architect	$24,700	$38,900
Bank Teller	$9,900	$15,300
Broadcast Technician	*	$23,569
Chiropractor	$28,000	$75,000
Computer Programmer	$29,500	$38,400
Dental Hygienist	*	$35,126
Dentist	*	$97,450
Drafter	$16,400	$28,500
Elementary Teacher	$22,500	$36,900
Firefighter	$19,760	$32,760
Flight Attendant	$12,700	$18,700
General Office Clerk	$13,000	$19,300
Hotel Manager	$30,000	$57,000
Insurance Sales Worker	$15,500	$31,620
Lawyer	$37,000	$115,000
Librarian	$28,300	$35,600
Optometrist	$55,500	$80,000
Paralegal	$23,000	$31,700
Photographer	$12,400	$25,100
Physical Therapist	$19,968	$37,596
Physician	*	$156,000
Podiatrist	*	$95,600
Police Officer	$17,900	$34,000
Postal Clerk/Mail Carrier	$25,240	$34,566
Psychologist	$39,100	$58,300
Registered Nurse	$20,540	$35,464
Secretary	$19,100	$26,700
Social Worker	$17,500	$30,000
Travel Agent	$12,990	$21,300
Veterinarian	$30,694	$59,188

No data available.

You may want to ask your parents how much they make, and how much money they receive each month after taxes are taken out. Ask them to show you how they budget their monthly salary.

As years go by, you will have to adjust your budget. You may have two salaries, children, a more expensive house, or school loans.

Another point to remember is that any extra money you have leftover is better off in savings. You never know when you will need it for car trouble, home improvement, or medical bills.

Whether you use the budget plan in this chapter or make one up yourself, the important thing is to work very hard to try and stick to it. Knowing your finances are in order will help you feel successful and proud of yourself.

Comparing Careers

Take time to look at a few high paying jobs held by men and women.

Lawyer	$115,000
Doctor	$156,000
Veterinarian	$59,188
Aircraft Pilot	$81,000
Computer Programmer	$38,400
Architect	$38,900

Listed below are common jobs held by mostly women.

Travel Agent	$21,300
Secretary	$26,700
Bank Teller	$15,300
Elementary Teacher	$36,900
Dental Hygienist	$35,126
Flight Attendant	$18,700

When you compare salaries between jobs for men and jobs for women, there is a remarkable difference, one that too many of us fail to recognize.

This information gives you a lot to think about, especially if you would like a more expensive lifestyle.

Money Isn't Everything

Earning a high salary can make life comfortable. However, keep in mind that it's important to like your job. Are you allowed to develop your talents? As I said earlier, you will enjoy going to work each day and you will also enjoy the people around you if you are happy at work. The money you earn is only part of your goal for a satisfying life.

What If I Don't Have To Work But Want To?

If you're married and you and your husband are employed, you may choose not to work. However, many women today are pursuing a career for reasons other than financial reasons. Staying at home all day with children may be unsatisfying and they may want a change. Some of their friends may have jobs that bring them a lot of satisfaction and personal fulfillment. Seeing this and reevaluating their own life may lead to changes about how they want to live.

Also, unfortunate things happen. Husbands die or lose their jobs, and divorces are more common today than ever before. An illness can also place a great financial burden on a family, and they may need more money.

Choosing to work full or part time allows you to keep up with the world around you. Workshops and on-the-job training help you become familiar with changes in your field and keep you aware of changes in computer technology. The knowledge you acquire will help you gain confidence, plus fill an emptiness you may feel being at home all day.

Whether you choose to marry or not, or stay home with or without children, is up to you. Decide on a lifestyle that focuses on personal success as well as your family's. If you give all of your time and attention to your family and forget your own needs, you will be very unhappy later. Your family will notice and it may lead to other problems such as jealousy and feelings of neglect and resentment.

Many parents and children today share responsibilities within the family. In some cases it's necessary for survival. One person can't do it all. People living in the family can decide who does what chores, how to share space for different activities, and how to allot free time for their friends or themselves. Chances are, everyone will be happier with a shared arrangement instead of having all responsibilities placed on one person.

Many women still stay home for a few years before picking up their careers. They may not have children, but decide to live a "stay at home" married lifestyle for their own reasons. There are also women who choose not to marry and remain single. Some even adopt a child and raise it without a husband.

You now have several things to consider when planning your future. Use the information in this chapter to put together a road map for yourself. It will guide you and help you become aware of the importance of a well planned and thought-out future for yourself.

Notes

CHAPTER

GOALS

I've mentioned that goals help you develop a purpose in life. I said that goals help you choose something meaningful to work toward and they give you a sense of direction in life. Having good self-esteem helps you attain those goals.

Believing that you are a worthy and capable person is a big factor when working toward your goals. If you feel confident enough to take healthy and reasonable risks, then your accomplishments help you become stronger as you decide what you want in life.

Setting goals is easy, but fulfilling them is more difficult. Like a dream or a wish, we set goals hoping to change something in our lives in order to improve it. Writing them on paper and making them happen can be challenging and fun.

Many people become successful through setting goals, because they are motivated and inspired to work toward something. Some of our most famous people provide good examples.

Walt Disney's dream was to create Disneyland. It was a long term goal. In his younger years, people laughed at his ideas and told him to take more "down to earth" classes in college instead of drawing pictures of mice and cartoon characters. Disney didn't listen to them because he believed in himself, even if others didn't. His desire was to see his dream come true, regardless of how many years it took.

He started by setting short term goals like getting a part-time job as an artist drawing pictures for greeting cards and other stationery. He then began to form his own small business. As time went on, his dream became a reality. He never gave up and because of his dream, people all around the world enjoy Disneyland and Disney World.

Walt Disney is not the only person who set goals and made his dream come true. Henry Ford dreamed of inventing an affordable automobile to replace a horse and carriage. He wanted average people to be able to buy cars, instead of just wealthy people. He invented the Model T Ford. Within a few years more and more cars became available, but Ford started the automobile "boom."

Thomas Edison invented the light bulb. His determination and drive changed the world. Remember: Edison also failed hundreds of times before he became successful.

When I asked my students what goals are, they said, "Something you want to do when you grow up." True, but goals are not only long term—something you hope to achieve when you're older. There are also short-term goals, those we try to achieve in a shorter period of time—a day, week, month, or year.

Let's look at some examples.

Short Term Goals	Long Term Goals
♥ To finish my homework before having free time.	♥ To find a part-time job in a career I'm interested in.
♥ To find something positive about each day.	♥ To attend college.
♥ To keep my room clean and organized.	♥ To travel to different parts of the world.
♥ To be courteous to other family members.	♥ To have my own family and live in a community where I can become actively involved.
♥ To try and do my best in school in all subjects.	

Sometimes people set goals and fail to reach them, because they don't do much to try and make them work. Or, because things get complicated they give up instead of working to overcome barriers. Much of this failure has to do with not being motivated to accomplish the goal.

But, if you need money to buy a used car, YOU'LL GET TO YOUR JOB; even if you have a cold or didn't get enough sleep the night before. Your motivation to get that car will help you get to work.

When one's motivation is not strong enough, it means that they don't care enough to work hard to reach the goal.

What Can I Do To Keep Myself Motivated In Order To Attain My Goals?

1. Talk with a friend, counselor, or teacher who is supportive of your goals.

2. Take time to think about positive reasons to reach your goal.

3. Visit with adults you admire. Ask about a time when they didn't think they would achieve their goals. Ask them to share ideas about staying motivated.

4.   If the goal involves a career, visit a workplace where you can see others working at this job. Seeing where your goal will lead you can help motivate you tremendously.

5.   Believe in yourself. Go back to Chapter 1 and read, "Feeling Good About Yourself."

It's a good idea to interview a person working in the career you wish to pursue. This helps prepare you when making decisions about classes to take and for handling working relationships with other people.

The following is an informal interview sheet that you may find helpful. Schedule a time with a boss or manager in your chosen career. Make a copy of the questionnaire and take it with you on your interview.

Interview Questionnaire For An Informal Interview

Name of Person _____ Date: ____ / ____ / ____

Job Title _____

1.   What interested you most about your career? _____
_____

2.   What courses in school helped you prepare for your career? _____
_____

3.   What were your biggest failures while studying for your career? _____
_____

4.   How did you correct them? _____
_____

5.   What do you like best about your job? _____
_____

6.   If you could change some things, what would they be? Why? _____
_____

7.   Looking back, are there any things you could have done differently? What are they? ____
_____

8.   What are some things I should know about working with other people? _____
_____

Is there anything I can do now to prepare myself for this? _____
_____

9.   How do you go about making important decisions? _____
_____

10. If you could start your career over again, what would you do differently? _____
_____

It isn't natural for you to be excited about your goals every day. There will be ups and downs. Writing down your goals will help remind you of your purpose for attaining them. It will keep you aware of your goals, and you'll believe that you can reach them.

Doing what you want and making choices and decisions are all part of setting goals. However, you should always consider your relationship with your family and friends. Try to set goals that will not cause conflict with them.

Goals That Reflect Your Values And Beliefs

You will need to set goals that reflect your values and beliefs. This means considering how much time you like being around your family, friends, and by yourself. It also means considering how much responsibility your parents trust you with.

If you spend most of your weekend time with your family, and you eat together Sunday after going to church, your goal may be to get a job that requires you to work Monday through Friday. Your family times come first. If you're involved with soccer and many of your practices are held during the week, then a weekend job might be better for you. Your parents may not allow you to stay out after 8:00 p.m., so you can't consider a late night job. They may not let you drive or have time to take you to your job, so you'll have to consider transportation.

When I was growing up, a boy in our school would stay with a ranching family many weekends in a row and help them with chores. We wondered why his parents let him stay away for so long and so often. As years went by, we found out that the boy's parents were alcoholics and fought a lot. The boy asked the ranching family if he could stay with them and earn extra money. Since the family knew how badly the boy needed to get away from his abusive home, they were more than happy to help him. In this case, getting a job and being in a healthy environment was more important for this boy's development.

If you were spending time with a friend whose family used drugs and they were using them around you, it would be better to choose another friend. Using drugs is likely high on your "no" list when considering your values.

Let's look at some things you should consider when setting goals. After all, if your goals aren't sensible and attainable, you will have a difficult time reaching them.

Most of your time is spent at home or in school. Your short-term goals will likely revolve around these areas of your life. Getting good grades is a short-term goal which will help reach a long-term goal of getting into college. Working part-time two days a week for a veterinarian can help you learn about the career if you choose it as your long-term goal. Helping with family chores teaches skills you will need as an adult. Answering the phone, taking messages, and learning to use the computer are skills you will need when working in any office or business career.

On the other hand, working as an assistant for a veterinarian would not be a good choice if you don't like working with animals or if you don't have an interest in pursuing that career. Helping in your uncle's law office wouldn't be a very good idea if the work hours prevented you from getting your school work done. Remember—your good grades will help you get into college.

You can see how setting short-term goals helps you reach your long-term goals. You must be sensible and weigh the pros and cons when you make decisions.

First of all you should balance your goals. Don't decide on goals that are focused only on school, or only on yourself.

SCHOOL	COMMUNITY
FAMILY	FRIENDS

Examples Of Goals That Are Good Choices:

1. *School Goals*	(a) I plan to finish my homework before 7:30 p.m. each day.
	(b) I'll volunteer in class more often.
2. *Family Goals*	(a) I'll help Mom clean up the house on Saturday mornings.
	(b) I'll spend more time with my baby brother.
3. *Community Goals*	(a) I will help with trash collection in the park in May.
	(b) I'll collect money in our neighborhood for a blood drive.
4. *Friend Goals*	(a) When Amy's not in school, I'll get her homework and drop it off.
	(b) I'll try to be a better listener when Amber needs to talk.

Examples Of Goals That Are Bad Choices:

1. *School Goals*   (a) I'm taking as many cooking classes as possible next semester, then I'll have to work less hard for A's.

(b) I'll do anything, even copy and cheat, to get a better grade than Mary.

2. *Family Goals*   (a) I'll stay home from school more often and watch the baby so Mom can get more rest.

(b) I won't change my clothes every day, so that Mom won't have as much wash.

3. *Community Goals*   (a) I'll work at the store longer and make more money even if I don't get my homework done.

(b) If Mrs. Nelson asks me to watch her dog, I'll say yes, get someone else to do it, and give them the money.

4. *Friend Goals*   (a) Jane can copy my work so I can help her get A's.

(b) I'll take drugs with my friends because they will like me better.

Balancing My Goals

1. *School Goals*

a. _____

b. _____

c. _____

2. *Family Goals*

a. _____

b. _____

c. _____

3. **Community Goals**

   a. _____

   b. _____

   c. _____

4. **Friend Goals**

   a. _____

   b. _____

   c. _____

If you're not sure whether your goals are good ones, ask an adult you trust to look them over and help you decide.

The following is an example of how you would go about forming your goals and sticking to them.

1. Write down a couple of long-term goals.

   ♥ To become an elementary school teacher.

   ♥ To travel to Europe someday.

2. Write down your short-term goals, following the steps in this chapter. Remember: While your short-term goals are helping you attain your long-term goals, you still need to set goals in the four areas (School, Community, Family, and Friends).

Example:

School Goals

♥ To do well in academics.

♥ To learn how teachers spend their day and how they present lessons.

♥ To have a counselor give me a survey to see if my personality fits with a teaching career.

♥ To learn a foreign language that will help when I'm traveling someday.

Family Goals

♥ To learn how to problem solve and communicate in a positive way with family members.

♥ To involve my parents in school activities.

Community Goals

♥   To volunteer at an elementary school in order to learn as much as possible about a teaching career.

♥   To interview teachers in order to learn the pros and cons of the teaching profession.

♥   To visit with a counselor and get information on required classes needed for teachers. Find out if I could support myself on a teacher's salary.

♥   To interview someone who has traveled to Europe.

Friend Goals

♥   To listen to my friends share their reasons for liking or not liking school. I may be able to make school more interesting if I learn what changes would make school more likeable for kids.

The goals listed are balanced for different areas of life, yet you are still working toward the future. Doesn't this make more sense than writing down meaningless goals that you won't stick to?

3.   Make time for your goals. Use the charts in the "School" chapter to help you plan and organize your tasks and interests. You're more likely to follow through if you write the tasks down.

4.   Remember your values and beliefs when setting your goals. If you don't feel right about what your plan is, it will never work and you won't feel happy, motivated, or confident about your life. This is extremely important when trying to attain your goals.

5.   Stay motivated. Always think of positive reasons for working toward your goal. If you are in a negative situation, try to think of positive things that come out of it.

6.   Don't cause conflict with your goals. If you plan to attend college but your parents can't pay for it, find other options. Ask your parents to look into a student loan. Find a part-time job that's right for you, or talk with a school counselor. Your parents are frustrated because they don't have the money, so don't blame them. Asking them to help you in other ways means you trust and love them—one of the nicest compliments you could give them.

7.   Write down what you have learned from your goal when you're ready. It's good to have results to look back on to see if you're growing toward your goal.

8.   Look over your old goals before setting new ones. Look at your comments about what you learned and accomplished. This will help you improve on your new goals.

My Goals

Long Term Goals

Date Completed

1. _____ _____

2. _____ _____

3. _____ _____

Short Term Goals

1. School Goals

Date Completed

a. _____ _____

b. _____ _____

c. _____ _____

What I have learned and accomplished: _____

_____

_____

_____

2. Family Goals

Date Completed

a. _____ _____

b. _____ _____

c. _____ _____

What I have learned and accomplished: _____

_____

_____

_____

3. Community Goals

Date Completed

a. _____ _____

b. _____ _____

c. _____ _____

What I have learned and accomplished: _____

_____

_____

_____

4. Friend Goals

Date Completed

a. _____ _____

b. _____ _____

c. _____ _____

What I have learned and accomplished: _____

_____

_____

_____

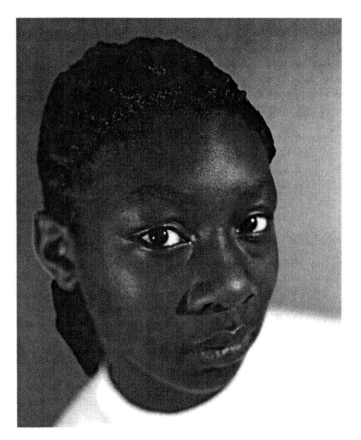

Save your goal sheets each year. If something you did wasn't successful, you can then change it or eliminate it. Some of your goals may be the same next year, and some will change.

What If I Don't Know What I Want To Do After I Graduate?

If you haven't a clue about your future plans, talk with a school counselor who can give you information about careers. Many schools, libraries, community colleges, and universities have catalogs, brochures and other reference materials telling you what jobs have the most openings and how much they pay.

One of the many benefits of setting job related goals is the experience you gain in a real life situation. This helps you determine whether or not you wish to choose that particular line of work.

Notes

Notes

CHAPTER

18

IT'S UP TO YOU

Making decisions based on values, understanding parents, resisting peer pressure, avoiding drugs, using my sexuality responsibly, caring for others, and setting goals. Wow!

You're probably asking, "How can I do all of this?" Well, you can, by practicing the life skills in this book.

You learned to walk, talk, and feed yourself from toddlerhood to now. These skills are easy for you because you practice them every day. It's much the same way while going through your pre-teen and teenage years.

Instead of learning to talk, you will learn assertive skills and communication skills. You will not learn how to put food into your mouth, but will become knowledgeable about good food to help keep your body healthy and drug free. Learning to walk was a struggle, but you did it, and learning how to play tennis is possible too.

You may even remember the first day of school. You probably put out your favorite clothes the night before and thought about what you would say to your teacher and the rest of your classmates. You will soon do the same when you interview for a job someday. What will you wear? What will you say to your boss and co-workers the day you report to work?

You will use many of the same skills you learned before you were seven years old. Your decisions will be more challenging, but you did it before and you can do it again. You can succeed.

It's up to you!

I wish you now and always only the very best.

Donna Ternes Wanner

Donna Ternes Wanner

Tell Me Now has been requested by individuals around the country. An updated version is now available for pre-teen and early teen girls to help guide them through the difficult years.

If you would like to share any experiences or write to me, my address is:

Donna Ternes Wanner
2214 Baldwin St.
Ft. Collins, CO 80528

Please include a self-addressed, stamped envelope if you would like an answer. Thanks.
Email address: teach22004@comcast.net

RESOURCES

Barkin, Carol, and James, Elizabeth. *Jobs for Kids*. New York, NY: Lothrop, Lee, & Shepard Books, 1990.

Bell, Ruth. *Changing Bodies, Changing Lives*. New York, NY: Random House, 1988.

Bingham, Mindy, et al. *Changes: A Teen's Journal for Self-Awareness and Personal Planning*. Santa Barbara, CA: Advocacy Press, 1987.

Bingham, Mindy, Edmondson, Judy, and Stryker, Sandy. *Choices: A Teen's Woman's Journal for Self-Awareness and Personal Planning (workbook)*. Santa Barbara, CA: Advocacy Press, 1984.

Bolles, Richard Nelson. *The New Quick Job-Hunting Map*. Berkeley, CA: Ten Speed Press, 1990.

Calderone, Mary, and Johnson, Eric W. *The Family Book About Sexuality*. New York, NY: Harper Collins, 1990.

Canfield, Jack, and Wells, Harold C. *100 Ways to Enhance Self-Concept in the Classroom: A Handbook for Teachers and Parents*. Englewood Cliffs, NJ: Prentice-Hall, Inc., 1976.

Canter, Lee. *Surviving Sibling Rivalry: Helping Brothers and Sisters Get Along*. Santa Monica, CA: Lee Canter & Associates, 1993.

Clark, Jean Illsley. *Self-Esteem: A Family Affair*. New York, NY: Harper & Row, 1985.

Clemes, Harris, and Bean, Reynold. *How to Raise Children's Self-Esteem*. New York, NY: Price Stern Sloan, Inc., 1990.

David, Jo. *Finishing Touches: Manners With Style*. Mahwah, NJ: Troll Associates, 1991.

Eagle, Carol J., and Colman, Carol. *All That She Can Be*. New York, NY: Simon & Schuster, 1993.

Earthworks Group. *Fifty Simple Things Kids Can Do to Save the Earth*. Kansas City, MO: Andrews and McNeel, 1990.

Fry, Ron. *101 Great Answers to the Toughest Interview Questions. 2nd edition*. Hawthorne, NJ: Career Press, 1994.

Gardner-Loulan, JoAnn, et al. *Period*. Volcano, CA: Volcano Press, Inc., 1981.

Goatman, Marilyn E. *When a Friend Dies*. Minneapolis, MN: Free Spirit Publishing, Inc., 1994.

Greenberger, Ellen, and Steinberg, Laurence. *When Teenagers Work*. New York, NY: Basic Books, 1988.

Harrill, Suzan. *Empowering Teens to Build Self-Esteem*. Houston, TX: Innerworks Publishing, 1993.

Hynes, Angela. *Puberty: An Illustrated Manual for Parents and Daughters*. New York, NY: TOR, RGA Publishing Group, 1989.

It Won't Happen to Me: True Stories of Teen Alcohol and Drug Abuse. New York, NY: Perigee Books, 1987.

James, Elizabeth, and Barkin, Carol. *How to Be School Smart.* New York, NY: Beach Tree Books, 1988.

Johansen, Sue. *Talk Sex: Answers & Questions You Can't Ask Your Parents.* New York, NY: Penguin Group, 1989.

Klare, Judy. *Self-Esteem: Looking Good.* Vero Beach, FL: Rourke Publications, Inc., 1989.

Lang, Denise V. *But Everyone Else Looks So Sure of Themselves.* Cincinnati, OH: Betterway Books, 1991.

Madaras, Lynda, and Madaras, Area. *My Body, My Self.* New York, NY: Newmarket Press, 1993.

Mason, L. John. *Guide to Stress Reduction.* Berkeley, CA: Celestial Arts, 1980.

Mayo Clinic Family Health Book. New York, NY: William Morrow & Co., Inc., 1990.

McCoy, Kathy, and Wibbelsman, Charles. *The New Teenage Body Book.* New York, NY: Putnam Publishing Group, 1992.

McElmurry, Mary Anne, and Bisignano, Judy. *The Changing Years—My Relationships With Others (workbook).* Carthage, IL: Good Apple, Inc., 1987.

McFarland, Rhoda. *Coping Through Assertiveness.* New York, NY: Rosen Publishing Group, Inc., 1986.

Rathers, Spenser, and Bougn, Susan. *AIDS: What Every Student Should Know.* Fort Worth, TX: Harcourt Brace, 1993.

Rich, Dorothy. *Mega-Skills.* New York, NY: Houghton-Mifflin, 1992.

Rosenberg, Ellen. *Growing Up Feeling Good.* New York, NY: Penguin Books, 1987.

Sanders, Corinne. *The Changing Year: My Choices and Decisions.* Carthage, IL: Good Apple, Inc., 1981.

Schwarzenegger, Arnold. *Arnold's Fitness for Kids.* New York, NY: Bantam, Doubleday, Dell Publishing Group, Inc., 1993.

Smith, Sandra Lee. *Setting Goals.* New York, NY: Rosen Publishing Group, Inc., 1992.

Stoltz, Sandra Gordon. *The Food Fix.* Englewood Cliffs, NJ: Prentice Hall, 1983.

Thomas, Alicia. *Self-Esteem: The Values Library.* New York, NY: Rosen Publishing Group, Inc., 1991.

Tiegreen, Alan. *Asking About Sex and Growing Up.* New York, NY: William Morrow & Co., 1988.

U.S. Department of Labor, Bureau of Labor Statistics. *Occupational Outlook Handbook. 1996–1997 Edition.* Lanham, MD: Bernan Press, 1996.

Youngs, Bettie B. *How to Develop Self-Esteem in Your Child: Six Vital Ingredients.* Ballantine Books, 1991.

Zerafa, Judy. *Go For It.* New York, NY: Workman Publishing Company, Inc., 1992.

Hotline Numbers

Teens and AIDS Hotline (nationwide referral service)	1-800-234-TEEN
KidsPeace (crisis intervention, information, and referral)	1-800-25-PEACE
National Runaway Switchboard	1-800-621-4000
National Youth Crisis Hotline	1-800-448-4663
Any Emergency	911

978-0-595-35445-0
0-595-35445-9

YOUNG ADULT

Printed in the United States
109295LV00006B/100/A